FLORIDA

Stories About Living the Good Life in the Sunshine State

Edited by Scott Tilley

Florida

Cover design © Scott Tilley

Front cover chair photograph © Fotoluminate LLC/Shuterstock

Front cover shuttle photograph © Everett Historical/Shutterstock

Back cover photograph © Henryk Sadura/Shutterstock

Published by the Anthology Alliance

**Anthology
Alliance**

An imprint of Precious Publishing, LLC

Precious Publishing
www.PreciousPublishing.biz

ISBN-13: 978-0-9996446-4-5
ISBN-13: 978-0-9996446-5-2 (ebook)

TABLE OF CONTENTS

DEDICATION

To all residents of the Sunshine State.

My parents didn't want to move to Florida, but they turned sixty and that's the law. – Jerry Seinfeld

PREFACE

Sunshine. Hurricanes. Disney. Alligators. Space. Pythons. Beaches. All are evocative of modern Florida: a mix of endless summer and destructive storms, amusement parks and deadly predators, invasive species and gateways to the final frontier. This is Florida today.

I live on the Space Coast, a unique area of east central Florida that is a narrow 72-mile stretch of Atlantic shoreline from Canaveral National Seashore to Sebastian Inlet. As the name suggests, the Space Coast is where the nation's space program began – and continues to thrive. I've seen Space Shuttle launches and landings, huge rockets taking off, and experienced the awesome scene of SpaceX's Falcon 9 boosters returning to earth. It's the only place I know where local hotels put three items on their beachside information boards: the air temperature, the ocean temperature, and the next launch time.

This anthology is a collection of stories about the sunshine state. From Miami to Jacksonville, Melbourne to Tampa, Orlando to Tallahassee, Florida is more than citrus, swamps, and mosquitos. It's about living the good life!

Scott Tilley
Melbourne, FL
August 21, 2018

Orlando, My City

By Christopher Adams

The best, the very best,
       way to appreciate this poem
           in your fingers,
    is to read it aloud.
Do not be concerned
    if others hear you.
Be boisterous and cheerful,
breathe deeply (periodically) and
---above all---
    laugh.

***

Orlando,
joyous city at dawn,
keeper of one gate
         through which our morning must enter,
good day to you,
    good day!

Orlando, poets' breath is lost at your beauty;
proud palm and striking oak
    o'er shadow me this day,
this dawn not yet here
    with the first chirrups
    of the unseen.

Orlando,
you are alive within me.
I sing of you as a haven,
as rest for my worn heart
         that arrived so weary with the world;
you refreshed me;
Yes, you!
You contain true love,
fair city.

True love
         sits here by your sheltering lakes;
in the midst of azaleas,
in bougainvilleas' shadows,
and, under the quiet scent of camphor,
         a glorious mix of roses reveals
         true love is here.

Why this effusive gushing
by a poet mad,
         delirious with joy?
Because,
there is also so much more to you,
city of life!
Yes,
dear city,

for within your gates

are the souls of this world
who reach for freedom
     and find it here;
who seek the kind hand of friendship
     and feel its clasp;
who cry for the dove of peace
     and hear its call.

Sweet town of my youth, grown up,
dear village gone,
great-wondrous and powerful city becoming,
these souls are within you
     and you hold them close.
"Orlando,"
they whisper,
     "Orlando."

Accountants, lawyers, bank employees...
all are here,
as are poets and sculptors
who yearn to carve their work
     with pen and torch
     within your boundaries.

Orlando,
I came to you as a young child.
An adult,
I am still that child,
but within you, I am not lost.

In this city of stunning color
and sublime poetry,
I am secure.

G-d is within you, Orlando;
        though I have traveled far and wide,
        though I have left G-d in other cities and places,
        I have found that G-d did not leave me at all:
this city teems with religious life.
The Christian,
the Jew,
the Muslim,
the Buddhist,
the Hindu,
the Baha'i,
the deist,
the Unitarian Universalist --
                all meet on the street to talk.

Why, yes,
my devout city,
within you,
        we meet.
One day, recently, we shared stories
        on the sidewalk in the bright weekend sun.
In view of your towering repository of knowledge,
        yes, in the wake of your library's journey into the
future,
                we secured the present...

4

our heritage of sharing earth with one another.

We, my city,
        held by you,
here touched our hearts together
and talked truths
we learned on G-d's knee...
here,
        in your borders,
        upon your land,
my city.

Why, why,
do I thus find you?
How do I see past your flaws?
Ah, good question;
good question, I say again
        as I inscribe this song to you,
        as I explode upon you with my enthusiasm,
        as I near burst this day with the happiness
                you have nurtured in me.

Why do I find you thus?
Question of questions:
why
        do I
                find you thus?

Because, in you,

Orlando,
I find every ingredient of life.

Every one!

Each single solitary one

piled amassed collected secured together
        yet, you do not hold them close.

No,
my beloved city,
you share them...
        with me,
        with the stranger,
        with the poor and the rich in heart.

Orlando,
quivering with the sun and blue sky,
you give of your self --
        we take, we build,
        and, soon, we, too, give.
We produce for you and your citizens;
we share as you have shared with us.
We open ourselves as you,
and we learn from you
the lessons you teach
at the banks of Lake Eola:
        we must take life within our hearts;

we must choose to grow.

Today, Orlando,
I wrote as you were speaking.
Beside Lake Eola, at six AM,
  I heard the ducks shuffle over grass,
  the carp's ripple by the southern wall,
  the robin's first call.
I saw the mirror of your lake
  capture the utter awe of the morning;
  your buildings, dressed in molten silica,
  also gripped distant fire.
Yet, both gave the dawn to me
  in ecstasies and joys that shuddered down my
spine.

Oh, Orlando!
You speak so clearly throughout my day:
  your city employees,
  your laundry workers,
  your citizens coming alive every new day --
    I hear their thoughts,
    I feel their hearts pounding.

Orlando,
as the day arises at Lake Eola,
the cobbled echoes from tires behind me
become to me your muscled stretching,
  your sinews twisting to life as you yawn.

Clowns and retirees
move closer to you;
singers and shopkeepers,
women who drive this city,
                    come to you;
parents who give dreams to their children,
these, too, seek you!

The enthusiasm of nations
          pours into you.
Orlando,
City of Lights,
city of open arms to the stranger
          and the traveler,

they all arrive seeking a bit of joy,
and it is here,
          now!
Oh, yes,
my proud city,
it is here.

For I find,
in Central Florida,
my dearest city,
                    you
          vibrant,
          effervescent,

glowing,
singing,
shouting,
joining with the stars
to smile and be smiled upon,
to burn and provide brightness,
and to lead with dreams.
So, with enthusiasm and joy,
I am always proud to stand with you,
this city in this wondrous nation,
and chorale fervently

My city, "my country, 'tis of thee...
of thee I sing."

# # #

Christopher "Kit" Adams has been writing since 1958. His poetry has been published from England to Hawaii, and poetry readings in Missouri and Florida have been well-received. A retired  Nationally Board Certified English teacher and National Writing Project mentor, he is a Fellow in the Space Coast Writers Guild and former President of Scribblers, a Brevard writing group. His first poetry collection, *Spanish Cedar, Preserving the ART of the Cigar Experience,* was released in March 2014.

THE AWESOMENESS OF FLORIDA HISTORY - AND GHOSTS

By Elizabeth Anderson

I've been teaching Florida History for over 20 years. I never tire of the exciting stories of our past and how we came to be the amazing place that over 116 million tourists chose to visit last year! Florida has so many things in its history that makes it unique. From Miami being the only major American City to be founded by a woman (Julia Tuttle) to the rich and diverse culture (Japanese, Spanish, British, Danish Greek and more) to the many "hidden springs" with underwater caves just waiting for you to discover, to the diversity of wildlife and nature, Florida just can't be beat!

When researching Florida's past, I found that I often came across myths, legends, and my favorite - ghost stories, that went along with the areas or people I was studying. I found that sharing these stories with my students seemed to help "cement" the historical aspects in their minds right along with the spooky stories I told. My students developed a genuine interest in learning more about the Sunshine State, and that made me one happy teacher!

There are thousands of stories of ghostly encounters in Florida, so I've chosen just a few of my favorites (ones that I've visited or experienced for myself), to share with you. I hope they will spark an interest in you to learn more about Florida, the Sunshine State!

Marsh Landings Restaurant - Fellsmere, FL

Fellsmere is a city in Indian River County. It has a high Hispanic population due, in part, to the surrounding agricultural industry, namely, citrus groves. Because of this, quaint little ethnic restaurants, unique gift shops, and other businesses thrive throughout the area. There is also a "cracker" history and the best place to see old photos and mementos of that era would be to visit Marsh Landings Restaurant! They are famous for their "Good Florida Cookin'."

I went to Marsh Landings because I heard that the food was incredible and the atmosphere was unique. I found the walls covered in local memorabilia and the food was, indeed incredible. With many choices of local cuisine, I chose the BLT with Southern Fried Tomatoes. WOW! My taste buds were in BLT Heaven! So, with great food and charming atmosphere, I foolishly believed that was all to be found at Marsh Landings. I was wrong! As my husband and I were enjoying our lunch, I noticed that the blinds seemed to have moved up a few inches. I shook my head and went back to my BLT. A minute later, the blinds were back down to their original position. I called the waitress over and inquired about them. "Oh, it's just our ghost." She explained calmly and walked away.

Intrigued, I looked further into this unassuming local restaurant. Built in 1926, it was originally a sugar company headquarters. Stories about visitors and staff seeing a young woman dressed in white and staring out the front window into the street have been reported.

The Florida Bureau of Paranormal Investigation has

done extensive work at Marsh Landings. After verifying reports from staff and visitors, they have recorded electronic voice phenomena (EVP) and captured ghostly photographs. Occasionally, they offer the opportunity for the public to attend "Dinner and a Ghost Hunt" at Marsh Landings. They have done extensive studies of the entire town and have persuasive evidence of paranormal activity, which they are happy to share with interested parties. (Florida Bureau of Paranormal Investigations Indian River Hauntings LLC 772-633-3955)

Ashley's Restaurant – Rockledge, FL

Ashley's is listed in the registry of haunted places. The spot where this restaurant stands is said to have been the site of an old railroad depot that burned to the ground. The existing building was constructed around 1932 and was called Jack's Tavern. It was an upper-class establishment where men wore tux and tails and ladies, fancy ball gowns. It thrived for many years while changing hands several times. Former names include Cooney's Tavern, The Mad Duchess, The Loose Caboose, Sparrow Hawk, and Gentleman Jim's.

When I first moved to Florida (around 1982), the Florida Today newspaper headline was "Gentleman Jim's Haunted." Coming from New York, where murder and mayhem dominated the news, I was enchanted that this was the headline of the day. I couldn't wait to visit! When I did, I wasn't disappointed. The outside is a fairly plain Tudor style structure with the definite look of a pub or tavern. Inside, however, is warm and inviting. There was a feeling of going back in time as you enter.

The food was excellent, service was wonderful, and on the table was a booklet – an excerpt from the Registry of Haunted Places telling the story of ghostly sightings at the restaurant. There were sightings of a pair of slightly transparent ladies' feet, dressed in old style shoes, showing under the bathroom stall door. When the door was opened, no one was there. Workers reported glasses being thrown from the bar, ghostly apparitions of a lady, floating down the stairs thought to be a girl named Ethel, who was murdered in the restaurant, and voices and flickering lights. While I didn't experience any paranormal activity, the "feeling" is definitely there! I returned many times since and the charged atmosphere is as stimulating today as it was when I first visited.

Ashley's Restaurant (Photo by Elizabeth Anderson)

Castillo de San Marcos – Saint Augustine, FL

I believe Saint Augustine to be the most haunted city in Florida. As a teacher, I have taken classes there each year for over 20 years. I love to teach Florida History, and with it, I always include the ghost stories that go with the different historical sites.

My favorite is the story of the secret room at the Castillo de San Marcos. The Castillo is the oldest masonry fort in the Continental United States. The first coquina stones that make up the fort were placed in 1672 and was completed in 1695. The fort remained under Spanish control until 1763 when a treaty signed Florida over to the British in exchange for La Habana. In 1783, it was returned to Spain, and finally, in1821, Spain ceded Florida to the United. In 1924, the fort was proclaimed a national monument.

Castillo de San Marcos (Photo from Pixabay)

While firing the canon off on the roof in 1938, there was a sudden cave-in, and the cannon fell through.

When they rushed downstairs to find it, they were stunned that there was no sign of the cannon anywhere. A worker with a lantern was lowered from the roof down to the cannon. What he found was shocking. First, the strong scent of a woman's perfume struck him. Upon investigation, the man discovered that this small room was completely sealed up with the skeletons of a man and a woman chained to the wall. Upon examination, carbon dating showed the skeletons dated back to the time when Colonel Garcia Mari came to take charge of the fort. He brought his much younger, beautiful wife, Delores Mari, with him. Delores was known for wearing a strong perfume to cover the unpleasant aromas that come with living in such a warm climate.

According to the tale, Delores was having a love affair with Captain of the Guard, Manuel Abela. The Captain was young, handsome, and exciting, all the things her husband was not. When Senora Dolores' husband, Colonel Garcia Mari, discovered the affair, he ordered the couple to be chained inside the gunpowder room and sealed them up alive behind a stone wall.

People often report seeing the ghost of Delores roaming the fort and leaving the strong scent of her perfume in her wake. I have visited this small room and have, indeed, detected the spicy smell of Delores' perfume. Though I have never seen her ghost, I have spoken to several workers at the fort who swear that they have. I plan to return many more times in the hope of meeting poor Delores and perhaps the handsome Captain Abela as well!

Mission of Nombre de Dios – Saint Augustine, FL

I was visiting the Mission with my eighth grade class one extremely hot May. I had shared with the students the story of a young Sister of Saint Joseph who had been a missionary to the local Timucua Indians. She contracted yellow fever and was buried with other members of her order on the grounds of the mission, right near the La Leche Chapel. After her burial, other victims of the fever who had been thought to be dead, actually "woke up" and recovered. Fearing they may have been hasty in burying this nun, they dug her up. To their horror, there were claw marks on the inside roof of the coffin. Her face reflected terror and her mouth was open wide as if screaming. Their great fear had been realized – she had been buried alive.

The young sister was buried again, but since that time, strange things have been reported by those who stand by her grave. A moaning sound seems to come from nowhere, and the ground underfoot seems to tremble. Perhaps it's phenomena reminiscent of her screaming and pounding on the coffin.

My eighth graders were utterly entranced by this story when I told it. When we finally arrived at the mission, we all went into the La Leche Chapel to pray. It was stifling inside, and two of my students began to feel faint. I allowed them to wander outside but warned them to stay within eyesight. They decided to stand by the grave of the young nun. Moments later, the girls came running and screaming to me as I stood in the doorway of the chapel. "She was there, she was there!" one of the girls shouted. Both were shaking and pale from fright. "What are you talking about?" I asked them. "The nun- it was the nun!" they told me. "We were standing by the grave when we heard the humming sound. The ground began to shake just like in the story!". "Let's go see," I said, believing that they had let their imagination run away with them.

While I do believe in the paranormal, I was convinced that the stories about this gravesite were mostly fiction. To my great surprise, when we stood at the grave, I heard the moaning. It seemed to be coming closer and closer. The ground was, indeed, trembling beneath our feet. My heart began to beat a little faster. I held the girls close to comfort them (and perhaps myself as well), and at that moment, a man driving a huge lawn mowing machine rounded the corner. He was the cause of the humming and the trembling ground. We all realized at once that he was our ghost and began laughing with relief. We may not have seen or heard a spirit, but we enjoyed a good scare!

Flagler College – Saint Augustine, FL

Flagler College is bursting at the seams with incredible history, and of course, ghost stories! I tell my students that when you enter a truly historical site, you are filled with a feeling of awe. Your senses become hyper-alert, you feel the hair on your arm start to rise, and a feeling of timelessness overcomes you. Some people attribute this to the presence of ghosts. I say it's history! I believe that history has energy left by the people who lived it. Maybe "ghost" is a good name to give it, but I prefer to call it "the awesomeness of history."

Flagler College (Photo from Pixabay)

Henry Flagler is known as the Father of Saint Augustine, Miami, and Palm Beach, FL. He was the key figure in the development of the east coast of Florida. Flagler built the Ponce de Leon Hotel, which was the play place of the rich and famous in 1888. It was known as the "American Riviera." Among the first guests were William R. Rockefeller, Frederick Vanderbilt, Mrs. Ulysses S. Grant, and President Grover Cleveland. Four other US Presidents would come to stay at the Ponce de Leon, as well as Mark Twain, Babe Ruth, Ernest Hemmingway, Robert Frost, and Marjorie Rawlings, to name a few. The hotel boasted fireplaces in every room, electricity, Tiffany stained glass windows in the circular dining room and luxury beyond compare. Flagler hired Thomas Edison to build the hotel's power plant. No expense was spared.

The hotel was eventually turned into Flagler College. What a fantastic place to get your education! Haunted by the ghost of Henry's second wife Ida (who went insane), students and guests report hearing her screams coming from one of the upstairs rooms. Flagler, himself, is said to stroll the hallways of the girl's dorms, smiling and nodding, making the girls feel welcome and safe there. Two female students told me that his presence is not frightening, but instead gives them a feeling of security.

Once, while visiting my daughter's best friend, whose dorm was upstairs right off the beautiful rotunda, a ghostly encounter occurred in the girl's bathroom. My daughter excused herself to use the restroom and came back a little shaken several minutes later. "I saw a little girl run into the bathroom. When I went in, she was standing by the sink. I thought it was odd because she was dressed in a very fancy, old-fashioned dress and had a huge bow in her long curls. She looked to be about four years old, so I asked her where her mommy and daddy were. I figured she was a sibling visiting an older sister. She ran into the stall laughing. I walked over to the stall and looked inside the door, which was ajar. No one was there! I looked all over the bathroom and she was gone." My daughter was puzzled because there was no way the girl could have left the restroom without being seen. Her friend just smiled and told us that this little girl was a frequent visitor. She is said to be a little four-year-old who died of a sudden illness while visiting the hotel with her wealthy family in the early 1900's.

Many more stories of paranormal activity at Flagler College exist. I suggest that if you ever get to visit the Ancient City, you put Flagler College on your list of "must see" places!

Walt Disney World – Orlando, FL

No visit to the Sunshine State would be complete without a stop at Walt Disney World! One of the most loved rides in the Magic Kingdom is the Pirates of the Caribbean ride. The ride was built in the 1970's. During construction, a loyal employee named George, a welder, passed away. After his death, fellow workers seemed to sense his presence at the ride. They fell into the habit of saying good morning and goodnight to George as they came on and off shift. They found that, if they forgot to do this, some strange things would happen during the day.

In the late 90's, one worker claimed to have seen George. He and a few other cast members were working the 3rd shift and decided to "walk" the ride. They had been joking about the ghost of George when suddenly the lights around them began to flicker on and off. A raspy voice was heard to say "You Need to Leave!" The men looked around, but no one was there. Seconds later, a man appeared in front of them, glaring, but saying nothing. They shined a flashlight to see who it was, but the light shined right through him. Terrified, the men ran. After they exited the ride, they commented on how the man wasn't actually standing; he had been "hovering" just above the ground. They were convinced that they had seen George, who was simply protecting the ride.

I've read about George before, and have heard that guests who say hello sometimes are treated to a flashing light as they pass a particular part of the ride, a message from him!

The Cassadaga Hotel – Cassadaga, FL

Cassadaga was known as "The Psychic Center of the World" at one time. The town boasts a population of mediums, psychics, spiritual healers, and channelers. The Cassadaga Hotel was built in 1927 to be a sanctuary of grace and charm. The hotel offers a lecture series, spiritual development classes, meditation circles, spiritual retreats, Reiki Healing and Color Therapy healing, group grief counseling, and private séances. Psychics and Mediums are available seven days a week to do readings, tarot card readings, past life regression, dream interpretation, and much more. There is a unique gift shop which sells books, candles, handcrafted items, and spirituality related items and services. I had an "aura photo" done there and it was remarkably accurate.

The Cassadaga hotel was once home to an Irishman named Arthur. He lived in room 22 and was quite fond of cigars and alcohol. Guests have reported smelling cigar smoke and catching a whiff of alcohol when and even feeling someone tap them on the shoulder when approaching the room.

Cassadaga itself is said to be inhabited by hundreds of spirits, drawn to the energy of the many psychics and mediums who live and work there. I've been told that it's not unusual to spend a few minutes in friendly conversation with a stranger you might meet, only to find out that no one else could see or hear that person, and you just had a visit from a ghost!

Miguel's Mexican Restaurant – Melbourne, FL

In the early 1980's in Melbourne, FL, Miguel's Mexican Restaurant served the absolute best margaritas on the planet! When I heard about them, I suggested a group of friends go after work on a Friday night. While we were there enjoying our frozen concoctions, I remember having the strongest feeling that someone was behind me at the table. I kept turning my head to check, but no one was ever there. At one point, I felt like a freezing cold hand touched my arm. I jumped up and spilled my drink. The waitress rushed over with a rag. I apologized profusely, and she told me, "Don't worry about it, it happens all the time. Touched, were you?"

She told us about all the strange things that happened in the restaurant, especially at night after guests had all gone. Glasses moved, chairs were pulled out from tables, doors opened and closed and just about everyone who worked there reported the same cold touch and feeling that someone was there behind them. Most frightening to me was that employees and guests reported hearing a little girl screaming when no child was there.

When I did some research, I found that Miguel's had originally been the home of a man known as Doc Sloan. He had been an infamous bootlegger during prohibition. In January 1920, the Eighteenth Amendment became law, banning the manufacture, transportation, importation, and sale of intoxicating liquors in the United States. This amendment became known as Prohibition. The people who illegally made, imported, or sold alcohol during this time were called bootleggers.

In 1926, Sloan's three-year-old daughter, Cora, accidentally set herself and the house on fire. The house burned to the ground, and Cora died. It is believed to have been Cora's screams that were heard by visitors. The house was rebuilt and eventually became Miguel's.

In 2003, the restaurant was torn down, and a CVS was built in its place. To this day, the ghost of Cora is said to haunt the location, and occasionally, a customer reports hearing a child's screams. This happens to be the CVS where I get my prescriptions filled. I've never heard a child screaming, but since I don't ever want to, I usually use the drive through!

***

Florida has a rich, action-packed history, and there are so many exciting ghost stories to compliment it! I hope these tales have sparked your interest, and that perhaps, you will travel around our amazing state to experience, for yourself, the awesomeness of Florida history – and ghosts!

# # #

Elizabeth Anderson was born and raised in Brooklyn, NY. She is a wife, mother, teacher, and published author. Her book, *Raising James*, has met with critical acclaim. She resides in Florida with her husband Rob and  their two dogs, Roscoe and T-Bone. She has two grown children, James and Hope. Her hobbies include writing, cooking, volunteering, and producing/directing murder mystery dinner fundraisers for non- profits.

28/80

By Lloyd Behrendt

"28/80...."

"What Dad?"

Ben Laren had not been paying attention and "the Col." saw an opening to exploit.

"28/80," the older of the two repeated cryptically.

"What's that, Dad?"

"It's up there, where we're headed," the newly-retired soldier/newly hired civil servant pointed up into the starry sky. They were on their way back to Paradise.

"Oh?" The younger man, his teenage son, was flummoxed. Just as planned.

"If you ever get lost, tell 'em you need to find 28/80. The Cape is smack there - Latitude 28W, Longitude 80N - easy to remember." Lt. Col. Paul Laren, the Cape's first Launch Weather Officer (LWO), talked with his son Ben, age twelve, on the riverside deck of the Motel Miami, 69th Street Causeway, sipping cherry cider, on a hot, muggy, Florida night, in June of 1960.

***

Benjamin Laren listened in amazement to the unexpected words as they ricocheted around his brain - words his friend Enrico, the video correspondent for the European Space Agency, uttered, on that unexpectedly cold February morning, at the Shuttle Landing Facility.

They were waiting for the normal double WHUMP as the Shuttle Columbia returned to KSC. Columbia was the Oldest Sister, the Grand Damme of the fleet.

STS-107 Launch - KSC Press Site SLC 39A

(Photo courtesy Graham Martin)

"Where are the sonic booms? I don't know, Enrico."

He inflected it into a question mark. It sounded like it came from someone else's mouth. It was one of those moments frozen in time.

"Where *are* the sonic booms?" His voice echoed in his head, too fitful to fill the silence.

"Columbia, Comm check..."

Shuttles always announced their return to the Kennedy Space Center right on time at T-3 minutes - three minutes before touchdown - with signature double sonic booms popping off the nose and tail. The shock waves were so close they almost sounded like one, as they shed enough energy bouncing through the atmosphere to land safely.

Amazingly, without any power.

This time, surprisingly, there was no arrival at T-0 to re-set the Universe. No BOOM! BOOM! No Columbia, STS-107.

Ben's mind slipped into *neutral* that blustery morning, as it never had before.

He wished never to go there. Ever again.

STS-107 Landing T + 5:49 - KSC SLF Mid-Point

(Photo by Lloyd Behrendt)

To this day, he is not sure what went through his mind before it recovered some semblance of presence. He knew this - across the last 35 Shuttle missions he had photographed landing at KSC, *every* Shuttle landed at T-0. Time and time again.

It was an amazing feat, to land that thirty-ton glider without any power and hit the same dime at the precisely appointed time.

No one would ever take that for granted anymore.

It was beyond comprehension to have an accident coming home.

Surely the danger was on the 'Up' side, at launch, with its "I-can't-shut-them-down" SRB's. The Solid Rocket Boosters could not be turned off once they lit, and that means they were uncontrollable during a failure mode. That was one in the chain of six or seven events that had doomed the shuttle Challenger years earlier.

Yet here they were. Back at another tragedy. The cosmic razor's edge of space cut way too sharp, way too deep, once again.

Space travel is unforgiving.

Columbia and the Crew of STS-107 were gone.

Columbia had tried her damnedest to bring her precious cargo home. She had even fired her vernier steering-only engines until they ran out of fuel, trying to right the horrible drag her broken left wing induced.

Nothing told her to. Her programs used "institutional knowledge" and figured out how to use jets that were only ever intended to fire in the vacuum of space to try and right the mortally-wounded bird. Yet F=MA rules physics with an iron fist. So, she ripped apart at 28,000 feet as she hit the atmosphere.

Does the Universe always win in the end? Is

apparent perfection rewarded with calamity to even out the scales in the long run? It wasn't a very comforting thought, but exploring space didn't come with a comfort guarantee then, did it? Or a guarantee of any kind at all.

***

Ben had been comfortable watching rockets happen, having grown up on the Space Coast. In the paradise underneath their ascending arcs, he learned how to surf on longboards as one of America's first surfers. Salad Days for sure. But he missed out on his ultimate dream - going to space himself.

He had pulled up lame, if you can call it that. While in AFROTC at the University of Florida, he needed glasses for nearsightedness. In 1970, that was a deal-breaker if you were trying to be a pilot.

His Liberal Arts degree was considered "non-rated" – not the same benefit an engineer or chemist would contribute prosecuting war. Especially *during* wartime. Although Vietnam was approaching its end, that was not yet evident.

On top of that, he had naively answered, honestly, when the Review Board for his commission asked why he had wanted to be in the Air Force. He'd told them he wanted to be in the Foreign Service and he thought joining the Air Force was a good stepping stone. These days, that would be called career path planning. Back then, not so. And Ben had neglected to tell them he meant after his Air Force career.

Had he known this was a barrier to entry, he would have said he wanted to be an Air Attaché. He just wasn't practiced enough to know the right buzzwords. They said they'd be in touch. How innocuous events can lever the Fulcrum of History.

He was never quite so crushed as when he got the "we won't be taking you" letter. Years later, when he recounted this trauma to a retired career officer, he was told with feigned surprise: "Oh, you told the truth!"

So, Ben didn't get to fulfill the legacy that all sons covet - to do what their Fathers did.

***

Panama Canal (Photo courtesy Lloyd L. Behrendt)

Ben's landing at 28/80 came on a warm October day in 1949, after his father, Captain Paul Laren, had taken the family for a Gulf Coast Drive - the car ride from New Orleans to Florida - after their boat trip up from Jamaica.

The debut destination for Ben's trip of life was the Panama Canal, the first Whistle Stop in his sojourn across the years. Ben had a connection along the way that wouldn't be famous for decades, and then would become grossly infamous: Gitmo - the holding tank for the cretins involved in killing thousands of innocents in New York City, September 11th, 2001.

Born at Guantanamo Bay Naval Air Station, almost-Ben, his mother Natalie, and her doctor barely made it from Vernam Field in Jamaica, where the Laren's were stationed, to the Naval Base in Cuba with its Big Hospital. The jaunt across the Straits of Cuba in a left-over B-17 made for precious little time after a late-night start, Ben's Mom having to leave an obligatory Officer's Wife's Cocktail Party early. The stork had his own schedule. They made it due to Natalie's fortitude, with moments to spare, so no B-17 birth, much to her relief.

B-17 (Photo courtesy Mike Killian)

On the return trip, the baby boomer came of air age at ten days old, already a world traveler, flying in a B-17 bomber that had just missed WW II, and then had been converted into a Caribbean basin Military Airlift Command transport.

Winging his way back home in the Flying Fortress, Ben was plunked on his mother's lap, in the aft bay's fold-down plywood jump seats. It seemed to him nowhere near as comfortable as his in-utero trip on the way over.

The "Nine-0-Nine," as the B-17 was later called when she was put out to pasture as a grownup Tony-the-Pony ride, was a memory quickly consigned to the impenetrable fog that all first memories get. Ben's was no different: the islands were solidly in the past - here was the Cape to discover.

He was *home* at 28/80.

Canaveral Lighthouse (Photo oil by Lloyd Behrendt)

Ben was barely beginning to talk when his mother Natalie took him and baby sister Sally down to the beach to watch the Bumper-8 launch, the first ever US ballistic rocket from the Cape. Bumper 8 consisted of a German V-2 rocket (captured along with Wernher von Braun at the end of the war) for its first-stage, and an American WAC Corporal (named after the Women's Air Corps) for its last second-stage, or propelled, section.

Bumper 8 Liftoff (Photo oil by Lloyd Behrendt)

Bumper-7 was slated to be the first. It had scrubbed for a mechanical problem and was bumped (ha!) into the dustbin of history. "3,2,1 ROCKET AWAY!" was the launch countdown back then. On July 24th, 1950, at 09:29 Hours, Bumper 8 took off from the Joint Long Range Proving Grounds (JLRPG).

The JLRPG was the Banana River Naval Air Station

during WW II, just a few years earlier. The Navy base and soon-to-be launch site would go on to become Patrick Air Force Base. It was named after the first Commander of the Army Air Corps, General Mason Matthew Patrick. Soon, it would garner a name worthy of legacies, imbued with the patina of cosmic relevance: Cape Canaveral Air Force Station. A cape that had been shaped by the first coquina clam, eons ago, and its random orientation, floating to the bottom, upon which American rocketry ultimately began.

The Missileer - July 31, 1950

(Image courtesy Lloyd Behrendt)

Ben had no recollection of this event, as he was just a year and a half old, but he had watched it, as his father tracked it. If the B-17 had been his cradle, then Bumper-8 was Ben's hobby horse. He was a true child of what was to become the modern 20th century. The world's first-ever space brat.

A few years later, his dad "The Col.," as Ben came to call him later in life, went to the South Pacific, solo, to become the USAF Weather Officer for the first test of an operational hydrogen bomb. At fifteen megatons, it was the largest American test ever, 1,000 times stronger than the WW II version atomic bomb. The mushroom cloud made 57,000 feet, 6,000 feet higher than Bumper-8 did on that July day four years earlier. Half as high as the WAC Corporal second stage, which made 125,000 feet at its highest point.

Operation Castle Bravo - 1954 (Photo courtesy USAF)

Ben's first look at a mushroom cloud was at that ripe

old age of 11 (having started school a year early, by then a sixth grader) when "The Col.," who was a Major at the time, was teaching Air Force ROTC at Louisiana State University. He brought Ben and Sally onto the campus on weekends sometimes, while he caught up on grading papers. If you ever saw any of the duck and cover B & W 16mm movies of fourth graders cowering under school desks, you'd understand and recollect Ben's early worries.

***

Between the rocket launch in 1950 and his father being shipped to Eniwetok for the H-bomb, life in sleepy Florida was pretty idyllic. Ben's memories are spotty and stream through his consciousness. The very first memory he could recall was in 1953 Eau Gallie, now part of Melbourne. The image was of playing with toy boats (wooden, as plastic was not yet common) in a Miami gutter - concrete curbs - on Orange Street in Loveridge Heights.

Other memories flow randomly. Breezy heat. Addictive protection of an Italian mother. The friendly German Shepherd next door. Black Widow spiders. The smell of naphtha from some plastic blow-a-bubble toys. A whip snake that frightened the kids and was dispatched after much weeping and gnashing, by the men. Being chosen to get a turn on the Car Lot Owner's lap at days end, steering the 1952 Plymouth or '53 Ford around the huge banyan tree in the middle of the circle at the Hay Apartments, named for Melbourne's first doctor. His first-ever fish on a line - a puffer fish at the Eau Gallie Library pier. Canova Beach. The beach, oh the beach. Before he got sidetracked by adulthood, while he was still a teenager, he would come to own that beach.

He also remembered being put in "jail" for the first time. It was his first run-in with cause and effect and the existence of consequences that he could recollect. They had been let outside to play, he and a little brunette girl his age, perhaps four, in the apartment's sandbox. He was never sure why he did it (except that probably she dared him, also beginning a pattern of being confused by girls), because one of Ben's faults was always to err on the side of being right. That was constant enough that it seemed to be part of his DNA. This time, however, he had poured a handful of sand down her white cotton panties, and in the imbroglio that ensued, Mama came down hard. He was grounded for the day (after he made a tearful apology to the young lady's mom, of course) and no amount of whimpering or batting of those brown eyes of his made any difference. The rest of the day went by in perfect Florida beauty, all alone outdoors with itself, while he had to stay indoors and be penitent besides.

***

In 1956, the remainder of the Laren family - Ben, mother Natalie, and sister Sally - would catch up with Paul in the Philippines. From there, it was off to Germany, where they fought the Cold War, flew home to the States, then on to Louisiana State University, where Paul taught a year of AFROTC, before he retired from the Air Force in 1960.

Around the world in 2,190 days.

The Laren family would do a Chinese Fire Drill, one last time. With their lives. It would again take them back to a place where they had been once before.

Cape Canaveral, Florida, U. S. of A.

28/80.

Canaveral Lighthouse (Photo courtesy James Brown)

***

The military was one of those double-edged swords. Retired out as a Light Colonel, Ben came to call him Col. out of respect for his service and his ethics.

The entity that had given Ben an experience by the time he was twelve that most people spend a whole life earning had shafted Paul Laren during the post-WW II drawdown. Even though he wanted to continue to serve, Paul Laren was mustered out. Ben came to learn that, as counterintuitive as it seems, politics, which are forbidden in the civic sense, were iron-clad in the military sense.

When Ben asked "The Col." why he retired in Melbourne, Florida, his father responded by saying it was the nicest place in an all-around way he had ever seen in his world-circling life. Of course, being from Milwaukee, you may notice 95% of his assignments in the Air Force were in tropical zones, so Melbourne fit in well with that –the tropics start in Vero Beach, only 30 miles to the south.

But in 1960, the home of Space Launch was not only charming and quaint, and very unpopulated - they had already lived there. Also, there was Patrick Air Force Base, with a commissary, a BX (or PX, the later term), a base hospital, and plenty of contractor and civil service work for someone steeped militarily.

"The Col." had forecast the first launch ever there. His work from then on would be bureaucratic; his gainful employment would not include weather, other than to wisely protect his family whenever there was a hurricane on the way.

***

Ben was beginning Junior High School, the seventh grade, and so got to attend a brand-new school: Southwest Jr. High. It was so named because it was in the then-southwest corner of the City of Melbourne.

Ben's sister Sally, in the fifth grade, two grades

behind him, went to Henegar Elementary in downtown Melbourne. It was housed in the first area schoolhouse, built in the land rush of the 1920's. The building was in the Roaring 20's-hip Mediterranean and Spanish Colonial Revival style made popular by Addison Mizner, an architect who settled in Palm Beach.

It was originally Melbourne High School and was named for Ruth Henegar, a long-time teacher and principal at the school. So, the distance between siblings in school foreshadowed their relationship through the years - miles apart. In distance, but not in love. Italian Mama Natalie always taught them blood is thicker than water, and they never forgot.

***

When you are twelve, what do you do with the rest of your life when you've already done that for which adults have worked a lifetime to accomplish?

Ben had circumnavigated the globe as a USAF dependent, courtesy of the good ole' US of A, visiting most of the historical touchstones of humanity along the way.

You do what any child unaware of such a feat would do. You keep going, one foot in front of the other, trying to inculcate your experience into the rest of things for your benefit. But none of that was apparent to Ben as he settled back into the American Way. Junior High was a reasonably decent place to do so.

Sure it was hard to leave your best bud every two years or so, but that is not like having to leave the boy (and girl!) friends that we make in that time between reaching adulthood and starting a family - high school and college days, if you were lucky.

Ben had scarcely hit the ground in the States and all of a sudden he was a *teenager*.

The Laren's had originally gotten a home in the new Mackle Brothers development named Port Malabar in the south end of Brevard County, also known for its Universe-class attribute, as the Space Coast.

Elliot, Robert, and Frank Mackle, and their General Development Corporation were responsible for opening up the central part of Florida in the aftermath of WW II. They sold lots to all comers for $10 down and $10 a month. Ultimately, the plan was for the lot owner to either relocate, or retire, to the Sunshine State, and build modest Mackle Bros. homes, where there had been none.

Their plan worked quite well. Florida began its journey to sprawl its way into the future, with homes popping out of the ground all over, from Palm Beach to Jacksonville. When the Laren's arrived back from their jaunt around the world, Port Malabar was ready-made to accommodate them.

***

A black mark that Major Laren had gotten back at Eniwetok, for neglecting to have a photographer to tout the conquering General in charge of the H-Bomb, followed him like a remora eel following a shark. He was mustered out against his will during the drawdown in the late 50's, trimming the personnel numbers that had waged the Big War.

First, they did half a year at War College in Montgomery, which prepared Paul to teach ROTC at LSU for a year. The latter was a holding assignment, one that filled the time he needed to reach 20 years, and retirement.

Not only was the Space Coast "the nicest place anywhere" according to the Col., but it was also chock-a-block full of good jobs with the government. After all, the United States had plunged into the Cold War, and the Space Race was on.

Paul Laren got one of those jobs with a government contractor, Aerospace Corporation, and later several civil service positions at Patrick AFB. It was not in the weather business; he would never go back to that. First, he was the Base Historian, and later the Real Property Officer on-base.

***

The Laren's moved to Port Malabar when it was a shadow of its future self. Many of those lots that were platted and sold from the 60's are still bare 50 years on, the development itself long gone, the Mackles having turned the sprawl problems and issues created as they enriched themselves, over to the people of the City of Palm Bay.

Back then, Ben got a paper route that gave him enough pocket money to buy a used 14-foot wood and fiberglass flat bottom crab boat, and a five horsepower Monkey Ward's Sea King outboard motor.

They would fish in Palm Bay, the real Bay, not the City - the Col., Ben, and Sally - one of the few times Paul interacted directly with his kids.

On their own, Ben and his pals would have "orange wars." There was a mostly neglected grove and a free-flowing 8-inch well on the site of the Bethesda "Old Folks" Home up on US 1. Two boys would be in the grove, they were the Army, and two in the boat, they were the Navy. Oranges were the ammo of choice, easy pickings, most of which had already fallen on the ground, too squishy to hurt.

Ben also learned how to sail in Turkey Creek, which runs into Palm Bay from the west. When the Laren's moved to Port Malabar, General Development still had a Yacht Club on the creek, and sailing lessons were a come-on to get people to settle down there.

Ben learned that if he could sail a pram, he could sail an America's Cup yacht. The physics were the same. Too bad he never pursued sailing; he was very good at it.

In 1960, the creek bottom was already covered with 3-4 feet of black gooey organic muck, a by-product of the runoff of developed lots, the place the water and the dirt used to stay put as nature intended. By the turn of the millennium, the creek where Ben learned to sail had turned into a solid island, covered with cattails and other vegetation.

The boys also used to take Ben's boat back up Turkey Creek, where it was still quite wild, for the sake of adventure. The most exciting discovery there was an alligator gar, a fish with a long snout and exposed teeth that made it look like a gator. The excitement part was when it broke water, it looked to be near as long as the boat, 14 foot. That area now is in the middle of civilization; any garfish, that big anyhow, are long gone.

***

Once Paul and Natalie got their bearings, they had a chance to scope out the area. Paul had settled in to begin, with a very secure job at Aerospace, and Natalie got a job as an Executive Secretary at the Radiation Corporation, later to become the Harris Corporation. These companies were part of the rapidly growing space industry.

The Laurens figured they would be there for a while, so they decided it was time to build a home custom designed for their particular needs. They picked up and moved out to "the Beach," as the barrier island on the east side of the Indian River (not yet recognized as a lagoon) was called by the locals.

Ben had been deposited two blocks from the real beach, the Atlantic Ocean, just when surfing was being imported by aerospace fathers who brought back used surfboards as they flew back TDY from California – which had just swiped surfing from Hawaii.

Ben's first board was a 9'4" Jacobs, shaped and fiber glassed in California by Hap Jacobs. It used to be a 9'6", but someone had dinged off the nose, and it had been re-glassed back on. His first day of surfing had started out poorly. At 5'2 and 100 pounds dripping wet with salt water, Ben had absolutely no upper body strength. He and his friends looked like the 90-pound weaklings who had sand kicked in their face, like the ads for muscle supplements on the back of the comic books they read.

When Ben and his buddies went out that first morning, the surf was "blown out." A strong on-shore wind created a large amount of chop to go along with some decent sized waves. The headwind made it impossible for any of them to even get "outside," far enough out to turn around and wait for a rideable wave without getting flipped over or sucked back by breaking waves, separated from their boards. There were no leashes in those days. If you lost your surfboard, you swam. All the way back in, no matter how far out you were. So, after many tries to catch a wave with no luck, they completely exhausted themselves. Having no other choice, they went and sat up on the beach to regain their strength.

Then something amazing happened. A mild cold front passed. The wind shifted from on-shore to off-shore, "glassing off" the surf, smoothing it out, and holding up the waves, so now the waves had pretty easily rideable walls.

Not even knowing how to cut, to turn sharply, they were able to crab their boards around and get some very decent and moderately long rides (longboards are made for that protocol). It was a quite an unusual circumstance on the sandy bottoms of the Atlantic Ocean. Florida's East Coast has no rocky bottoms, no points jutting out into the sea that you find in those other places, Hawaii and California, that shape and make waves more rideable. The boys were hooked.

Ben Laren, a world traveler, had now added another title to his young life: surfer. It was the beginning of a life-long love affair with his first girlfriend - Mother Ocean.

***

Ben was still math-challenged. It was unclear whether it was caused by head trauma of an early-in-his life sledding accident in Germany - he was forced into a tree by a friend who thought it was funny - or by a phobia created by the embarrassment he was put through by his fifth grade teacher, who sent him to the blackboard and forced fractions on him when he didn't even know what that slice of a number was. The real reason will remain unknown. The result was that he had to take a different elective than the rest of his Space Age classmates, who at least acted like they got "new math."

It just so happens that this key deficiency would scribe the rest of Ben's life, although at the ripe old age of twelve he had no clue.

The elective that fit his schedule was a graphics art class, taught by the school's shop teacher, Mr. Kalimar. Sheldon Kalimar was a hidden treasure in the shop: a photographer schooled at the New York Institute of Technology, world-renowned for teaching the art of hand-colored photography.

Ben would never call it that. To him, they were oils-on-silverprint, a technologically-proper description of the art form in which painting black and white photographs - silver prints - with transparent oil paints, transformed them into color images. The technique was the first-ever form of color photography, dating back to the 1800's, before the chemistry creating Kodachrome,

46

the first color film with a stable red dye, worked out by Kodak in the 1920's.

To Ben, it seemed as if the "hand-colored" designation sprang from others looking down their noses because the sketch was from a camera, instead of being done with the charcoal that painters of oil on canvas used. No one ever called those hand-painted oils, did they?

Before the advent of digital images, and giclees (from the French, to squirt, which came to mean to paint with drops of ink), wasn't all art done with hands? So why, Ben wondered, were oils on canvas not called "hand painted canvases?" He would come to learn the world of art is full of snobbery, but it still always ticked him off. In fact, given his subject matter (he would do many, many pieces of rocket launch art) he was proud of the fact that he could not alter the reality of the moment except for the color palate. In that fashion, his work was as real and historic as any image ever could be, and not the subjective art that "hand-sketching" allowed.

The school at which Mr. Kalimar studied was the ultimate in teaching the oils-on-silverprint technique, anywhere, the New York Institute of Technology. So the shop teacher, when allowed to teach a graphics art class, went with what he knew, with gusto. As a result, Ben learned the technique that would be an artistic enhancement for black and white film. Ironically, he was using horse and buggy technology to capture images of rocket-science technology.

It was also a *unique* means to do art that emulated

the avian art of another artist who graced this coast of the Land of the Flowers. It just so happens it was the same stretch upon which Ben had been planted: the Space Coast. The artist was none other than John James Audubon.

In 1834, Audubon made it down to the northern reaches of what would become the Space Coast. He was intent on the scientific capture of flora and fauna from the American wilderness. Centuries later, Ben became an acolyte of JJA's, when he discovered the connection. Ben had taken up keying on birds in much of his artistic work to continue Audubon's work, and for several other reasons.

Firstly, birds' ability to escape the bonds of earth and soar separated them from other animals. Given his heritage and love of flight, that freedom naturally appealed to Ben.

Secondly, his early mentor in black and white photography, David Daley, was a big fan of birds. Dave was an experienced photojournalist who shared a darkroom with Ben in Ben's first-ever job in the real world: working at *The Melbourne Times* newspaper, in the days of B & W-only newspapers. Ben saw a lot of bird art as he was coming up.

Thirdly, while working at an art gallery in downtown Melbourne, Ben learned that half the fine art purchased (in the mid-1990s anyhow) featured birds as subject matter. So, seeking to make a living with art, which he rarely/barely did, he chose to try a bit of customer service and give the customers (so he thought) what they wanted.

When he discovered that Audubon, who was fastidious about getting birds in their natural environment, was working in the same place where Ben lived, he polished his portfolio with an emulating bird series. Later, in the marshes behind his studio, he befriended a pair of precious sandhill cranes that became real friends and put his bird art over the top.

The third leg of Ben's artistic stool, to go along with rockets and birds, was historical work that he originally called "Vanishing Florida." As time went by, Vanishing did not seem quite right, so he would come to call his third defined series "Emerging Florida," much the way the peninsula had risen from the seas eons ago, and never really stopped morphing in one way or another. It was changing rather than vanishing, and since Ben loved puns, he chuckled at using a geological term to describe changes that continued to lift up the Land of the Flowers.

***

The universe had set Ben's "life top" spinning.

After 6 years as a preschooler in the 50's Florida, at Patrick Air Force Base, his schooling went like this: Kindergarten, Buffalo, New York, 1954. 1st and 2nd grades, Clark Air Force Base in the Philippines, 1954-1956. 3rd, 4th, and 5th grades, Ramstein Air Force Base in Germany 1956-1959. Second half of 5th grade, Montgomery, Alabama. 6th grade, Baton Rouge, Louisiana, 1960.

In the summer of 1960, the top finally wobbled to a stop back at Patrick Air Force Base.

With a secure future set in motion and easier to divine, the family moved up from the modest Port Malabar home on the mainland, to a still modest but larger home with a pool, in Melbourne Beach, only two blocks from the Atlantic Ocean. It was a nicer neighborhood, and also closer to work for the Col., as Patrick AFB was also on the barrier island.

For Ben, it meant an ocean within walking distance, five minutes away even if you were carrying a longboard.

Back then, no one would cut school to go surfing. Early on, surfing did not have the "Fast Times at Ridgemont High" reputation it would later acquire. Ben had moved on to life before that happened. For now, life was good – and seemed to be getting better.

***

It was now 1961.

It was before Viet Nam…

It was before the assassinations…

It was before drugs…

It was at the outset of the sexual revolution…

Now only a year away from teenager, Ben was as unaware as a 12-year old would be about the coming storms.

He and his dad would joke about putting up a wall at the Georgia border with machine guns on top, to keep out the hordes that were coming to build and fill all those exurban homes that the Mackles had foisted on

Florida.

Years later, Ben wished they had taken their own advice. Florida's 1960's 5,000,000 souls would swell to 16,000,000 in 2000, and 21,000,000 by 2017.

It would be some trip, and Benjamin, the world traveler by age 12, was in it for the long haul. After moving every two years or so in elementary school, he was not leaving his home and friends ever again if he could help it. He would be staying... at 28/80.

# # #

Lloyd Behrendt was born at GITMO.  He watched the first US rocket take off from Cape Canaveral in 1950. A University of Florida PCL grad in 1970, he began his photographic career with Apollo 17 and has since photographed 450 Cape launches. His books *STS-135 Covering the Last Shuttle Ever* and *Raising Crane - Sandhill Cranes in the Marshes of Malabar* can be found at http://www.amazon.com/author/lfb.

FLORIDA HAS IT ALL

By Anne Bonner

Florida
Fun in the sun
Pristine beaches high-rise hotels
Restaurants theme parks sports games
Cruises missile launches
Disney World fantasy
Dancing with fairies magical pixie dust
Gobbled by dinosaur monsters
Lost in Star War's galaxy
Old Florida
Revitalize restore your soul
Everglades "River of Grass"
Marshes swamps cypress knees
Slash pines palmettos Sabal palms
Great blue herons snowy egrets ibis
Indigo king invasive boa python snakes
Air boat rides marveling at nature
River of Grass fantasy
Floating on a puffy cloud
Gliding on a gator's back
Flapping in the air like a wood stork
Heaven on earth
Florida

# # #

Anne Bonner is a fifth generation Floridian. She grew up in Cocoa, attended the University of Florida, and lived all over the world as a military wife. Florida is the recurring theme of  her ten historical fiction books: five novels and five Y/A books. She judges poetry contests and her recent release is a book of poetry, *ENJOY! New & Selected Poems*. An artist, Anne paints the covers of her books. More information about Anne is available online at www.annebonner.com.

GERMANS TROOPS IN FLORIDA DURING WORLD WAR II

By Gene Davis

Did you know there were German Combat troops in America during World War II? They were infantrymen, tank commanders, aircrew, support personnel, and submariners. They were not, however, active combat troops – they were prisoners of war (POW).

At the peak, in May 1945, there were 371,683 German POWs in the United States. Florida, according to one source, had 11,746 prisoners. There were 700 camps in 45 states. There were two main camps in Florida: Camp Blanding near St. Petersburg, and Camp Gordon Johnston on the southern part of the Panhandle. Camp Blanding, at its peak, had 20 branch camps.

Prisoners in Florida were housed in two main camps: (1) Camp Blanding: Banana River, Belle Grade, Bell Haven, Clewiston, Dade City, Daytona Beach, Drew Field, Green Cove Springs, Homestead, Jacksonville, Kendall, Leesburg, MacDill Field, Melbourne Naval Air Stations, Orlando, Page Field, Venice, and White Springs; and (2) Camp Gordon Johnston: Dale Mabry, Eglin Field, and Telogia.

How did the United States end up receiving German POWs? The first prisoners entered Camp Blanding, in Starke, Florida, on September 24, 1942. They were crewmembers of German U Boats sunk in the Atlantic Ocean off US shores. Interestingly; crewmembers of the *Graf Spee*, a German battleship scuttled in the harbor of

Montevideo, Uruguay, were also part of the POW contingent.

The US initially resisted receiving European POWs, but the lack of Allied-controlled territory in Europe, and the limited space in England, which began to house American GIs, led the US to finally accept the pleadings of British Envoy to the State Department, Lord Halifax, in August 1942, to receive German Prisoners of War.

The US Army Office of the Provost Marshall General (the OPMG) was given responsibility for implementing the POW program for an initial estimate of 50,000 prisoners. The count of POWs reached 54,502 in July of 1943. The battles in Africa with Rommel's *Afrika Corps* quickly ensured a doubling of POWs interned in the US. By the time of the November defeat of the Germans, the number of POWs in the US was 122,350.

German POWs were transported to the US in returning troop carrier ships. Somewhat ironically, given the number of US ships sunk in the Atlantic, not one of the ships carrying POWs was sunk.

The prisoners were housed on military bases, in former Civilian Conservation Corps Camps, in specially built POW camps, and even some in the Santa Ana Racetrack in California. There is no record of the prisoners running or betting on any races there.

The OPMG was given the goals of:

1. Abiding by the 1929 Geneva Convention on the treatment of Prisoners of War (signed by both the US and Germany);

2. Ensuring treatment of the German POWs was such it encouraged fair treatment of US prisoners in Europe at the hands of the Germans; and

3. Developing a labor program to address a severe labor shortage in the US caused by the recruitment of many American youths for military service.

The US was scrupulous in adhering to the provisions of the Geneva Convention to the extent that when facilities were not ready for POWs and they lived in tents, the US Commander required his personnel to also live in tents, despite barracks being available for the US troops. The treatment of German prisoners brought media and Congressional criticism at various times and places throughout the US.

On the second goal, despite some atrocities committed against US prisoners by the Germans and the adverse war environment in which US prisoners were held – especially in the later stages of the war – US prisoners, especially in camps run by the Luftwaffe, were treated in a marginally acceptable manner.

Conversely, our adherence to the Geneva Convention concerning German POWs may have helped the Allied cause. For instance, General Dwight D. Eisenhower, the senior US military spokesman in Europe, told Congress: "[I] was able to drop safe-conduct passes by the millions over enemy lines, promising treatment per the Geneva Convention, causing a considerable number [of Germans] to surrender."

The third goal, "development of a labor program using POWs," was exceptionally successful.

The OMPG, under the Army Services Forces, ran the POW program through Nine "Service Commands." Florida's POW camps were under the Fourth Service Command, headquartered in Atlanta.

While US Forces (Army and Navy) controlled POW camps, POWs themselves were subject to the command of German NCOs and Officers, even though officers and enlisted were segregated in different camps.

The camps and prisoners were monitored by the US State Department, the International Red Cross, the International YMCA, and a Swiss Legation representing Germany.

The "Nazi" and "Anti-Nazi" nature of the camps led to internal conflicts among the POWs, even to the point of prisoner's deaths caused by fellow POWs. Fourteen Germans were tried at the end of the war for the murder of their fellow prisoners.

Control of the prisoners was usually maintained with a corps of US enlisted men who "guarded" the prisoners on about a 1 to 10 ratio. Later, some of the prisoners working on farms were guarded by roving patrols alternating between the various work sites.

Early concerns about the prisoners centered on potential escapes and sabotage. There were no references that I found to any real sabotage – although there were occasional work stoppages.

The two primary uses of POW laborers were in tasks

on US military bases and support of all phases of American agriculture. By November 1944, there were 74,000 prisoners employed in agriculture and 69, 899 on military installations. By November 1945, however, 115,369 prisoners were engaged in agriculture with probably the same number on bases as before.

Prisoners were employed in everything from timbering to canning plants to citrus harvests to being mechanics, laborers, laundry-men, and even watch repairers. One site stated their German watch repairman was much quicker and better than anyone else available. The POWs are credited with building the swimming pools at Melbourne NAS and Banana River NAS.

Only enlisted POWs were required to work – and could not work in war industries or hazardous activities. Non-Commissioned Officers (NCOs) could only be made to supervise. Officers could not be made to work. Some volunteered anyway to get away from the camp environment.

Florida had, perhaps, the best and worst labor camps. The best was Kendall near Miami. POWs served as gardeners, mechanics, electricians, painters, kitchen helpers, and also as hospital workers in the large Miami hotels, requisitioned as locations for recuperating American soldiers.

A visiting Red Cross inspector observed: "This camp is the best looking we have seen. ... The prisoners are fully aware of the privileged situation of the camp, and they take good care of it."

On the other hand, the nastiest camp was probably Clewiston, Florida. The labor force there harvested sugar cane. Red Cross Representative Guy Metraux described the camp as "a flat, treeless region and very dry. There had been no rain for six months. ... The heat was continuous – 103 degrees on the day of my visit. ... The camp, located in the middle of a sugar cane field, held prisoners engaged in the incredibly hard work of cutting cane in snake-infested fields."

An interesting side note: Germans were fascinated with snakes, hunted them and made belts and wallets – to take home as souvenirs.

Prisoners were paid eighty cents a day, in addition to ten cents a day for essentials such as toothpaste and soap. They were paid in script which could be used to buy articles in the Base Exchange or to take home as hard currency at the end of the war. The primary purpose of the script was to ensure prisoners did not have local currency to use in escape attempts.

The US government collected the fair wage of the POWs (nominally four dollars a day). The residual, after the worker's eighty cents was deducted, went to pay for administration of the POW program.

Officers, though they didn't work, were paid a salary. Lieutenants received $20+ a month; captains, $30+; and majors through generals, $40+ a month. In addition to being paid, German Generals led somewhat privileged lives. They had single quarters, an aide-de-camp, and sometimes a staff which might include cooks and a gardener.

It's estimated POWs contributed over 90 million worker-days on military installations alone from 1943 to 1946 at a value of approximately 131 million dollars. That does not include the value of freeing US personnel for duty in the war. Given the earlier figures of double the POWs working in agriculture as compared to those on bases, you could probably estimate the POW contribution in the private sector as twice that earned on bases.

The farmers and industries using the POW labor lamented its loss when the POWs started matriculating at the end of 1945.

German POWs were usually well housed and certainly well fed, especially compared with the diets of US prisoners in Germany. One German prisoner stated: "When I was captured, I weighed 128 pounds. After two years as an American POW, I weighed 185. I had gotten so fat you could no longer see my eyes."

The following menu, published in the *West Orange News* and served in one of the Florida camps, brought criticism that the POWs were being coddled and certainly were getting better diets than US citizens on rationing. The POWs were served:

- Roast beef with gravy, veal loaf, baked ham

- Pork sausage, barbequed spare ribs, turkey ala king, roast veal with dressing

- Boston cream pie, French Toast, fruit salad, white cake with chocolate icing ... and coffee, milk, cream, and butter (I'm sure you remember or were told by your parents or grandparents about oleo margarine – you had to self-color it, and it didn't taste like butter).

The *News* concluded: "So, these Nazi rats who have fortunately fallen into the tender hands of our military forces are eating as good food as our service men ... and much better than our civilians can obtain under rationing restrictions."

For a POW engaged in the labor program, the following might a typical day:

- Reveille – 5:30 a.m.

- Breakfast – 6:00 a.m.

- Return to Barracks – 6:30 a.m.

- Work start –7:30 a.m.

- Lunch – noon (often furnished by farmers or a lunch from the camp)

- Return to work – 1:00 p.m.

- Cleanup/Return to Camp – 4:30 p.m.

- Dinner – 6:00 p.m.

That's a better schedule than I had as an Air Force Academy Cadet.

There were, nonetheless, work stoppages. At the camp at Telogia, Florida, in August 1944, the POWs in the logging camp refused to work. When the entire camp had its rations reduced to bread and water, however, they went back to work.

The Clewiston Camp, mentioned earlier, was the site of the only documented suicide. Karl Behrens, a young soldier, escaped from the camp in late December 1944. He was found by the FBI early in January in a tree, having apparently hung himself.

In all, there were 2,200 escapes throughout the US. That is about 1/3 of one percent of the POWs, less than the percentage of numbers of escapees from US prisons. Florida had 33 escapees, least of all the states. Most escapees were captured within days or weeks, usually because of hunger. There were two exceptions: Rheinhold Pabel escaped from Camp Grant, Illinois, in 1944 and was not captured until 1953. Georg Gartner escaped from the Camp at Deming, New Mexico, on September 21, 1945, and gave himself up on the *Today Show* in 1985, 40 years later.

Why were there so few escapes by the German POWs? There are probably four reasons.

1. First, the environment was not conducive to escape. There was no place to go, and in the south, there were dogs and aggressive sheriffs.

2. Secondly, the work program occupied many of the prisoners and gave them an outlet from camp life.

3. Third, there were extensive programs at the camps from libraries to craft shops to musical/theatrical involvement and productions (surprisingly one of the most favorite records was *Don't Fence Me In* by Bing Crosby)

4. And finally, the US POW environment was rather benign. Many of the soldiers (particularly those not ethnic Germans) were happy to be out of the

war, reasonably fed and clothed, and treated within the provisions of the Geneva Convention.

With respect to entertainment and off-duty time, there was an incredible array of activities and events, especially at the larger camps. Camps had libraries of English and German books. Most camps had projectors and an inventory of movies, screened by US personnel. There were camp orchestras and bands, with scheduled performances. Theater groups did plays from *Faust* to *Cyrano de Bergerac* and skits – probably not unlike the sailors' show in *South Pacific.*

An established education program was so good it was recognized formally by the German Government as legitimate college work. The returning POWs received German credits toward college degrees.

The sports programs were extensive and well organized – centered, naturally, on European football – soccer. There were competitions and championships. Many of the activities were watched not only by German officers but by American personnel as well.

Almost every camp had a newspaper, which was surprisingly uncensored, at least early on. The content was used to judge the local POW temperament. Later on, when the US began a re-education program, the papers were watched carefully and a "national" paper was produced by German writers and editors – with guidance from US advisors.

While there is extensive information about the various camps in Robert D. Billinger, Jr's *Hitler's Soldiers in the Sunshine State,* I found little information on the

POW detachments in Melbourne, Florida.

We do know that several POWs worked in the administration and mess halls of the POW facilities. However, most were engaged in manual labor, such as operating the "night laundry detail."

Why isn't there much information available on the Melbourne NAS and the Banana River NAS camps and limited information on some of the other sites? Firstly, the Government significantly limited the information available to the media and the American public on the POWs.

Certainly, the farmers and industries that employed the POWs knew they were here and were grateful for their help. The only time news of POWs was actively promoted by the government was when there was an escape. I found no evidence of escapes from the Brevard facilities.

Secondly, in Melbourne, for instance, the 296 prisoners -- 148 at each base -- were employed in duties on the bases. As noted, they may have done significant work such as building swimming pools, but their work wasn't publicized.

What type of work did POWs perform on bases? A wide spectrum of duties. They worked in personnel, as clerks, infirmary orderlies, dental clinic aides, tinsmiths, on mosquito control, as mechanics, tailors, and shoe repairmen. They served in laundries, did manual labor work in construction, and worked in mess halls.

We know quite a bit about several locations because the International Red Cross and YMCA representatives, per the Geneva Convention, visited the camps and rendered written reports. It is these reports that labeled Florida sites as the "best of camps" and the "worst of camps."

There is no question that Florida played a crucial role in the German POW story. From the best to the worst camps to housing some of the initial prisoners from submarines, Florida was in the middle of activities involving the POWs.

Conversely, German POWs had a large, positive influence on Florida. Their use in agriculture, from citrus to sugar cane harvesting to canning to forestry activities kept these industries from collapsing. The use of manpower on military bases reduced, as it did in agriculture, the negative impact of the loss of our productive workers to the war effort.

What happened to the POWS after Victory in Europe on May 8, 1945? Other than the two cases noted above and the 860 who remained – in cemeteries – all of the German POWs were sent back to Europe.

Not all, however, were sent to Germany. Many went to England and France and remained POWs for an extended period of time. Many did not want to return to Germany as their homelands were now under control of the Soviet Union.

Numbers began declining in June 1945. Extradition of all German POWs was completed in July 1946. Given their importance to the citrus industry, some of the last POWs to leave were in Florida. The departure of the Germans ended an extraordinary story – one not known by many Americans.

In Florida, none of the prisoners, despite their appreciation of the Sunshine State and their treatment here, were allowed to stay after the war. There is evidence, however, that former POWs did return, some to settle here permanently.

References

1. *Prisoners of War in America,* Arnold Kramer, Scarborough House, 1979.

2. *Hitler's Soldiers in the Sunshine State,* Robert D. Billinger, Jr., University Press of Florida, 2000.

3. *Florida in WWII: Floating Fortress,* Nick Wynn & Richard Moorhead, 2010.

4. *German prisoners of war in the United States* – Wikipedia.

# # #

Gene Davis is a Life Member and Past President of the SCWG. He coordinated the Guild's Children's Writing Workshops and Contests for several years. He authored chapters  and helped edit "Sea Turtle Five" for the SCWG's children's serials in *Florida Today.* Gene served on the editorial board and wrote reviews for SCWG's *Literary Liftoff* magazine. He authored *The Kissing Camels* and *Murder at the Blue Ridge BBQ Festival.* Gene and his wife Judy have two children and seven grandchildren.

UNRESPONSIVE

By Dan Fisher

The first of July started out like any other summer day in Florida. Drizzly most of it. "No reason I can't ride this afternoon," he said to himself. "The weather's not too bad." He was headed to university classes in Cocoa, about 40 miles north on Interstate 95. He had made the trip many times. He worked the midnight shift, 11:00 p.m. to 7:00 a.m. On these work nights, he would go to classes in uniform to save time and ensure he got to work on time since classes ended at 10:00 p.m. and it would take nearly an hour to get to the police station. Many cops did that; it was common to see officers from many local departments in full uniform on any given night.

Around 4:00 in the afternoon, he got "booted and suited" in his uniform: dark blue, with a large, shiny badge over the left shirt pocket. Then he put on his helmet, rain suit, gloves, and boots—all covering his uniform. He was all set. He grabbed his law books, tossed them into the rear carrier, before hopping onto the motorcycle and riding off into the weather.

He would muse when he'd pull up at a red light next to some little old lady in inclement weather. Invariably, she would look over at him with a look that said, "Oh, that poor young man. He must be wet and very uncomfortable!" Far from it. He dressed so that he would stay dry, even in the worst weather that Florida could throw at him.

"I'll bet that I'm drier than she is," he would say to himself. He figured that she had to run out to her car in the rain, ditch her umbrella in the back seat, then get into the driver seat. By this time, she would be soaked. He, on the other hand, almost always got suited up indoors and walked out into the weather—much like an astronaut getting ready to venture outside the Space Shuttle.

He merged into traffic on the highway and slowly got up to an appropriate speed. He always rode more slowly in bad weather. He knew he had only two tires instead of four, and of course, there was no steel cage around him like in a car. Having seen many traffic crashes in his career, he knew well what his fate could be if he weren't careful.

The ride up the Interstate was more or less uneventful. Even at this late hour in the afternoon, traffic wasn't too bad. He knew where all the potholes and other pavement imperfections were. This stretch of roadway had been built over 25 years ago. It had been resurfaced a few times, but time and weather always take their toll.

As he rounded the wide curve about a half mile from his exit, he saw what Floridians know as the "gray wall of water" up ahead. The rain comes down so hard it looks like dark gray and black streaks ahead. Sometimes, when there's a wind, the lines seem to curve, instead of coming down straight. "Oh, crap," he said. He wasn't worried; he had ridden in that kind of rain before. But, he knew that it was going to be a nuisance. He would have to slow down and exercise even more care than he had been. "Thank you, Lord, for nudging me to leave a bit early."

That was the last thing he would say. As he rode out from under the overpass, which gave him some respite from the pouring "gully-washer," a bolt of lightning came crashing down. His body stiffened with the million or so volts of electricity coursing through his body. Then, he went limp. His bike went one way, and he went another. He was what first responders call "unresponsive"—no heartbeat, no breathing. For all intents and purposes, he was dead.

He lay on the ground for several minutes. People began to gather, wondering what to do.

"Is he dead?" one passerby asked.

"I don't know," said someone else. "It sure looks that way."

An elementary school teacher came up. She had been trained in CPR but had never been called upon to put this training into practice. She hesitated, trying to recall what they had taught her in class earlier that year. "I've got to get this helmet off him," she said. "There's no way I'm going to get any air into his lungs with it on. She fumbled with the strap until she figured out how to undo it, and then removed it. THUMP! His head hit the pavement. "Oh, my, now he's probably *really* dead," she thought.

Just then, another woman walked up. "I'm a cardiac nurse at the hospital. Is he breathing?" She took charge, which gave the teacher a sense of relief.

"I don't think so," the teacher said.

As they looked at him, lying on the side of the road, other bystanders began holding pillows and blankets over the victim and the rescuers. "Give him breaths when I tell you to," she said to the teacher. "One thousand one. One thousand two. One thousand three..." She continued that cadence for a minute, then said, "Give two breaths. NOW!" The teacher breathed two long breaths into the officer's lungs. The nurse and teacher continued their back-and-forth for several minutes. At one point, a doctor from the emergency room showed up. He relieved the nurse, who was beginning to grow weary. She took over the rescue breathing from the teacher.

This was long before cell phones were in everyone's pocket. People began to wonder how they were going to get an ambulance to the scene—if that would even be necessary. They still thought that the man on the ground would more likely need a morgue than a hospital. Suddenly, another person showed up. "I'm the public safety radio technician and a trained paramedic. What do you need?"

The freed-up teacher shouted, "An ambulance! We need an ambulance. Right now!"

The radio tech went to work. Since he was the countywide radio tech, he had radios to contact every public safety agency in the county. He picked up a microphone and said, "Radio maintenance calling Sheriff's Department. Radio Maintenance to Sheriff's Department."

"Sheriff's Department, go ahead, radio maintenance."

"There's a man down on I-95 at Fiske Boulevard. He's unresponsive. CPR is in progress. We need Rescue and Ambulance immediately!" You could feel the tension in his voice. His sense of urgency was greater than it might normally have been. He had caught a glimpse of the victim and thought, "This man looks familiar."

"10-4, radio maintenance." We're sending a deputy, a rescue unit, and ambulance."

"Thank you. Radio maintenance clear."

CPR continued on the hapless officer—whom no one knew *was* an officer, since he was still in his full rain suit. "What's going on, here," the doctor wondered out loud. "I'm not getting good chest compressions.

"Yes, I was wondering the same thing," replied the nurse. It's almost like there's something on him to prevent us from giving him good compressions." They took a moment to reassess the situation. "I see a zipper on this rain suit," continued the nurse. As she unzipped the outerwear, they saw the badge pinned to the victim's chest. "Oh, my word, he's a police officer!" They ripped open his shirt and discovered the culprit—the officer's body armor. Meant to protect his life in case of attack, it wasn't doing him any good, now.

They also saw the burn marks on his clothing, and they saw the fabric of the bulletproof vest through the burned outer covering. With the vest out of the way, they were able to provide better chest compressions. However, they still weren't able to get a pulse. The officer continued to lie unresponsive on the ground.

In the meantime, a small crowd of people had gathered to watch. The rain poured down on all of them. Lightning flashed all around. Many strikes were frighteningly close to the scene. It was as if some evil spirit was hell-bent on making sure that this officer would not survive the day. The onlookers seemed just as determined to breathe life back into the officer. People brought out blankets, pillows, and sheets of plastic that they had stashed away in their cars to shelter the rescuers.

The sound of sirens could be heard in the distance, then closer. The Sheriff's Department car arrived just ahead of the ambulance and rescue squads. The deputy sheriff walked up. "Who is he?" she asked. When she saw the officer, she continued, "he doesn't look very good, does he?"

The doctor looked up and just shook his head. "We don't know who he is, but he is a local police officer." The deputy pulled a handheld radio from a pouch on her belt and said something into the microphone. Something about a Medical Examiner's report. She was convinced, based on the amount of time since the original call came out, and who knows how long he lay on the side of the road before the call came out, that this officer would be taken away in a body bag.

The rescue crew took over CPR. People continued to shelter the officer and the rescuers from the blinding thunderstorm. They could shield them from the rain, but the lightning continued relentlessly.

"I have a pulse!" someone shouted. A cheer came up from the bystanders. Then, "I lost it. Damnit!" They put the officer on a gurney and handed his wallet and personal items, including his gun belt, to the deputy. She put everything into her car. She picked up the microphone of the car's two-way radio and said, "Bravo 47 to dispatch."

"Bravo 47."

"10-4. I need you to call the Palm Bay Police Department and let them know that lightning struck one of their officers. It's Badge Number 90. He doesn't look like he's going to pull through."

There was a noticeable pause at the other end, the kind when any public safety professional receives word that a police officer is in dire straits. "10-4, Bravo 47. We'll make the call."

"Damn!" the deputy thought. She wondered about the officer. Was he married? Did he have any children? He seemed fairly young. She checked his driver's license and did a rapid calculation. "Thirty-three years old. I'll bet his parents are still alive." She wondered whether they lived in the area.

***

It turns out that they did. His wife would be notified, and she, in turn, would call his parents—and hers. They all gathered at the hospital. They waited, and waited for some word, "No news is good news," said his mother, trying to sound upbeat. But, being a nurse herself, she knew that the chances were slim that her son would survive.

The paramedics rolled the gurney carrying the lifeless officer into the ambulance. They cut off the remainder of his clothing and marveled at the damage the lightning bolt had caused. His shirt was in tatters. His pants had holes burned in them where the million or so volts of electricity did their damage. They wired the officer up to the monitors. Nothing. The officer was "flat-lining," as medical people describe a person with no pulse. The EKG display shows a solid horizontal line instead of the familiar waveform of a beating heart. They all shook their heads somberly as they continued chest compressions and breaths. They weren't going to give up without a fight!

The hospital was about eight miles away, but with the relatively low speed the ambulance had to travel in this blinding rain, it might as well have been a hundred. Finally, they pulled up to the entrance of the hospital. The doors opened, and the officer was wheeled out of the transport unit and into the emergency department.

Modern ambulances are very well equipped—much more so than they were even a few years before when a patient would be hurriedly put inside and rushed to the hospital. They now are virtual mobile emergency rooms, with much of the same, state-of-the-art technology that a hospital ER would have. However, even with all this going for them, the actual ER is much more efficient and conducive to restoring life.

Inside the ER everyone was geared up. The medical staff worked relentlessly on the near lifeless officer. "Thank God, someone who knows CPR stopped and worked on this guy," one nurse said.

Another replied, "I heard she's a cardiac nurse."

A third replied, "Wow, that's amazing! What are the odds of that?"

"What are the odds of someone getting hit on a moving motorcycle, and then having a cardiac nurse stop to render CPR?" A brief silence followed as they all took in the significance of that question.

Nurses and doctors shouted at the officer. "Hello! Can you hear me?" "You were struck by lightning!" "What day is it?" "Who is the President?" All the standard questions that are asked of a patient to determine his or her level of consciousness and/or brain damage. The hapless officer mumbled a few incoherent words, but nothing that would indicate he was back among the "land of the living."

Finally, someone exclaimed, "He has a pulse!" A quiet cheer went up from the medical staff. They continued asking him questions to try and keep him coherent. "Where are you?"

"Hospital," came the feeble reply.

"What's the name of the hospital?"

"Worst off. That's why I feel so bad."

"It's Wuesthoff, but that's okay."

"Do you know what happened to you?"

"I was tchruk."

"You were what?"

"Tchruk."

"No, you weren't shot."

"No. Tchruk!"

"Struck?

"Yes."

In between times, the officer was screaming out in pain, which was excruciating. Perhaps the most pain a man could endure. They turned him to examine him for injury. There was a burn running from his right shoulder all the way down to his waistline—and below. It was then that they had time to notice the odor of burned flesh emanating from his body.

In the meantime, the officer heard a voice—a gentle, quiet, male voice. "You were hit by lightning."

This statement made sense to the officer. He didn't understand why, but it just did. It sort of explained things—put them into perspective, possibly. "Am I going to die?" He wasn't worried about dying. It was more of a question of "what's next?", rather than a sense of foreboding.

"No, you're not going to die." the voice said.

The officer understood. Just as he wasn't afraid of the possibility of death, he also wasn't relieved hearing the "good news" that he was going to live. It was all like an academic exercise, almost as if they were discussing someone else. As though he, as an officer, would be discussing the fate of a victim of a crime or other calamity.

When he was stabilized, the attending ER physician visited the officer's wife. "He's had a terrible experience.

We had a rough time keeping him alive. We nearly lost him two or three times. He's stable, now."

"Oh, thank you, Doctor. Is he out of the woods? What is the long-term outlook?" She didn't even know what to ask. This type of injury was all new to her. Would her husband ever be the man he was? Would be able to go back to work? Would he have a disability for the rest of his life? The answers to these, and many questions not even thought of, remained elusive at this early hour in his recovery.

***

The officer was sent home after a week in the hospital. He spent months at home recuperating. His chest hurt from the CPR. His back ached from the healing burn, and his muscles were in a constant spasm. The extreme electricity from the lightning had short-circuited his entire nervous system. He suffered from fatigue. His wife took him to the local mall one day. They walked from the car to the mall entrance, and then perhaps 25 yards into the mall. That was enough. He was spent! She got the car and took him home.

Slowly, he recovered. He finally got strength enough to go back to work—light duty, office work, but he was able to work a few hours a day. When he arrived that first day, he received a standing ovation. "We're glad you're back!" said one officer. Another said, "We were really worried about you." "Let me see your burned-up uniform," said yet another!

Many months later, the officer recalled the conversation he had had with the unidentified man.

"You were hit by lightning," "You're not going to die," and the resultant total lack of emotion. He realized that he had no recollection, whatsoever, about the chaos and confusion in the Emergency Room. That was confusing to him since, in his experience moments like this in the Emergency Room were loud, boisterous, and chaotic. Certainly, if he recalled this quiet, almost whispering voice and conversation, how much more should he remember the commotion in the ER? That's when it struck him. It was **not** a medical person he had been conversing with! He had been speaking with his Creator!

#

Dan Fischer was struck by lightning on July 1, 1986 and had a full and miraculous recovery. He served for 26 years with the Palm Bay, Florida Police Department. He was born in Kissimmee,  Florida, long before Disney World and the other attractions were even a thought. Dan is a graduate of University of Central Florida with a bachelor's degree in Legal Studies. Thankfully, Dan is still alive and well, and married to the love of his life, Joanne. He lives in Palm Bay with Joanne and their two Dachshunds, Wally and Ozzie.

VICTORIA'S DOLL

By Joanne Fisher

The aroma of coffee seeped into Charles' bedroom. He closed his eyes and deeply breathed in the aroma of his favorite brew. His morning Joe was almost finished when he entered the kitchen. He looked out the window and noticed that the sky was a beautiful robin's egg blue, without a cloud in sight. He was acutely aware that the weather could change on a dime in Florida. Floridians have a saying, "If you don't like the weather, stick around for ten minutes and it'll change." Even though Apalachicola is in the Panhandle and flirts with freezing temperatures in the winter, it's still Florida in the summertime, and an afternoon thunderstorm is always to be expected. The rain didn't bother him at all. He welcomed it, especially since the temperature would drop dramatically and freshen the day.

He headed out to the trailer park where he had an inspection scheduled. One of the older trailers had caught fire a couple of days earlier, and after the initial cleanup, it was up to the Fire Marshal to make the final determination of the cause and file the paperwork for the insurance. Unfortunately, mobile homes do not have good payouts from insurance companies, due to their construction and perceived value. Charles had a heart for the residents of this rural county and always did his best to make sure his inspection would turn into a decent payout for the owner. Hopefully, they could buy a new trailer without having to dish out a substantial amount from their pockets. Unless it was arson; that was a different story. He had no mercy for people who torched their own home for an insurance payout.

While he was driving, a call came in from Toni. He hit the talk button on his headset.

"Hey, Sweetie!" Toni said with an alluring voice.

"Hey, lady! What's going on?" he asked.

He had been seeing Toni for a little over a year, now. He liked her, but she definitely wasn't the love of his life. She was very beautiful, but she was shallow and selfish. Initially, he thought he could add some humility to her, but he was sadly mistaken. She kept hinting at marriage, but he always promptly changed the subject. She was a nice lady, but not marriage material. He wanted someone who was kind, altruistic, caring, and patient. He knew well that this person would be hard to find and most of all, he also knew well that Toni was not the one.

"Nothing much. I was wondering if you had thought about what we talked about the other night at dinner."

Oh, yes. She wanted to meet his parents. That was out of the question.

"Yes, I thought about it, but I don't think I'm ready for that step yet."

"Oh, I see. Okay. I'll see you later, then." She hung up.

He could tell that she was miffed. It didn't bother him. He would deal with her later.

He arrived at the "Four Winds Mobile Home Park" around nine. He parked his truck and walked towards the site. As he approached, he noticed that the fire had damaged the front of the trailer, which meant that something probably had happened in the cooking area. He noted that on his notepad and shot some photos. He carefully opened the door and climbed in. He continued to take notes and take pictures of the damage he found. At first, he noticed the burn was very bad around the stove and he thought it was from bad meal preparation, but then he slid on the floor and almost fell. There was an oily substance on the floor. He took more notes. He slowly made his way to the back of the trailer and noticed that it was in reasonably good shape. Yes, there was slight damage from the smoke but, all in all, the back was intact. As he went to turn and go back to the kitchen area, he hit his foot on a trunk. He heard a cry coming from the chest. He froze in his tracks, his adrenaline pumping!

"What the—!"

He unlocked the hitch on the truck and lifted the lid. There, lying on top of some old clothing, was a perfectly preserved porcelain doll! She was almost two feet tall with reddish long curly hair, big dark eyes, light porcelain skin, wearing a light pink, lace dress with white lace trim, similar to the styles of the Nineteen Twenties. She was a beautiful doll, perfect in every way. He had never seen anything like it. He wondered how it could be so perfectly preserved. Perhaps the trunk was lined with metal, and that protected the doll and the other toys inside the trunk from fire damage. He picked her up, and she began to sing:

"Ring around the Rosy, a pocket full of posies, ashes, ashes, we all fall down!"

"Well, aren't you an amazing little thing," he said.

He held her up for a few seconds and thought, surely, a little girl was missing her doll. She most probably went through a traumatic experience with the fire, and now she's missing this doll. He knew that the little girl would wonder about the fate of her doll. Well, she was saved, and he was going to bring it to her. He placed the doll back in the trunk and closed it. He picked it up and hauled it to his truck.

As he finished placing the trunk on his back seat, the next-door neighbor came out.

"Good Morning Ma'am."

"Good Mornin', sad, ain't it?" She asked.

"Yes, it certainly is."

"Are you a fireman?"

"I'm the fire marshal, ma'am. I'm here for the official inspection."

"Oh, I see. Such a tragedy! I hope those stingy insurance companies pay her what is due to her! She's a single mom, works very hard, you know. I watch her daughter for her, you know."

"Oh, really?" he thought. Perhaps she knew where he could find the little girl. "Do you know the little girl's name?"

The lady's face lit up. You could see she was fond of that child.

"Victoria is her name, and her mother is Flora. I'm Doreen. Nice to meet you," she said as she extended her hand for a handshake.

"Good to meet you too, Doreen, I'm Charles. Fire Marshal Charles Ford," he said as he shook her hand.

"Between you and me, Marshal, I think Flora could use a hand right now. She and Victoria are homeless. They're staying at her parents' home in Tallahassee, and she's still working at the restaurant in Apalachicola. Her commute is brutal!"

"I see. Well, Doreen, thank you for informing me. I found something in the trailer that belongs to Victoria, and I'd like to return it to her. Do you have her grandparents' address by chance?"

"No, sorry, Marshal but I do know where Flora works. Would that help you?"

"Oh, yes, very much so."

"She works at the Restaurant Prairies Vertes."

"Oh, yes, I know where that place is. Thank you, Doreen; I'll go over there now."

What a nice young man, Doreen thought. She wondered if he was married. "You're quite welcome, Marshal. Good luck, and remember what we talked about," she said as she gave him a wink. He knew well what that meant.

"I will." And he took off.

As he drove, he became excited. He knew that Victoria would be thrilled to hold that doll in her arms again. He always enjoyed the look on children's faces when he was able to return their favorite toy to them.

Sometimes, he would buy the same toy if he found it was badly damaged and replace it altogether. The children would ask him how the toy was saved, and he would tell them that it was just a tiny miracle.

When he arrived at the restaurant, it was still closed. The lunch rush hadn't begun yet, but he saw the hustle and bustle inside. He knocked. He noticed a tall, stocky man come to the door.

"May I help you?" he asked through the window.

Charles pulled out his badge and placed it against the glass. The door was unlocked immediately.

"How can I help you, officer?"

"Marshal. Fire Marshal Charles Ford."

The man nodded. He was large, but he seemed nice.

"I've come to see Flora. Is she in?"

"Oh yes, the fire. So sad. Please come in and grab a seat. I'll go see what she's doing. Would you like a cup of coffee?"

"Yes, thanks, I'd like that." Charles sat and began looking at all the wall hangings without any interest at all. He was thinking about his report and how to word it so that the insurance company would pay out a fair amount to Flora.

"Hi there," she said.

Charles turned and beheld the most beautiful woman he had ever seen. He was mesmerized by the beauty of her red hair, freckled skin, and the sexiest voice he had ever heard. This was the one! She was the woman he'd been waiting for. She was perfect, and he had just met the love of his life.

"Yes, h-hello, I-I'm Charles Ford," he said with a stutter. "Oh, that's Fire Marshal Charles Ford. I-I'm the fire inspector." What? He couldn't even speak! Oh my! This was going to be a tough one! He couldn't fall in love now. He had to do his job first. Stop it! Charles! Stay focused!

"Oh, hello, I'm Flora Mantovanelli. I'm the owner of the trailer," she said as she shook his hand.

Charles felt something in that handshake. The warmth and spark confirmed that she was the one. He didn't want to let go, but he did.

"Um—I'd like to speak to you outside if you have a few minutes."

"Of course," she said, as she headed back towards the kitchen. "Jimmy, I'm going on break for a few. Is that okay?"

"Sure, Flora, that's fine."

She headed towards Charles and began removing her apron. "Where are we going?"

"Oh, just outside." He said as he opened the door for her. Like a distant bass drum, thunder was playing its midday song.

Since he parked his truck a block away, they had to walk towards it.

"So, how long have you been working here?" he asked.

"Going on my fifth year. I love this place and love the people! Jimmy is a great guy! Where are we going?"

"Oh, just to my truck. I have something for you— actually for Victoria."

"Oh? How do you know my daughter's name?"

"Doreen. We met when I was at your trailer for the inspection."

"Oh, Doreen. Yes, she's a pearl. Victoria adores her."

"Yes, and I'm pretty sure Doreen adores both of you," he said as they reached the truck. Charles reached inside, pulled out the trunk, and laid it on the sidewalk. He opened it and removed the doll.

"Oh my God! It's Rosie!"

"Is that her name?"

"Yes, Victoria named her because of the song she sings."

"Makes sense."

"B-but how did you find her?"

"She sang to me. Seems like she wanted me to find her so that she could return to Victoria."

Flora began to cry. She took Rosie and hugged her. Charles pulled out his handkerchief and handed it to her.

"Thank you." She dried her eyes and remained silent until she composed herself. She leaned against the truck and began to stroke her long curly hair.

"Rosie was a Christmas gift from Santa when

Victoria was nine. I had bought it on layaway, but just a week before Christmas a layaway angel went to the store and paid off the remaining balance. Good thing she did, because I had no money left. Oh, I remember that Christmas morning when she opened the package. Victoria was beside herself, jumping for joy and giggling because every time she jumped up and down, Rosie would sing her song. I'd never seen my daughter so happy!"

"I can see why. This doll is beautiful."

"Yes, she is."

Then Charles had a thought.

"Would you mind if I gave her the doll personally?"

He thought that he could use the opportunity to get Flora's address.

"No, I wouldn't mind, but we're living in Tallahassee right now, and it's two hours away—on a good day!"

"It doesn't bother me. I would drive all night to see the look on your daughter's face."

"All right. If you say so," she said as she looked for something to write with.

Charles pulled one of his business cards out of his pocket and handed it to her.

"Here. You can send me a text message with your parents' address," he said as he packed up Rosie and placed her back into his truck. "Let me walk you back."

"Oh, you don't have to."

"I insist."

"Wow, this man certainly is a gentleman," Flora said to herself. "Not like Victoria's father, the deadbeat." He had taken off only a week after Victoria was born and never sent a dime in child support. Flora had tried to contact him many times, but he never picked up her calls. They always went to voicemail. A couple of years later, he changed his number, and she never heard from him again.

Charles opened the restaurant door for Flora and said, "Don't forget to text me, okay?"

"I won't. Thank you, Charles!"

"Don't mention it; it's my pleasure."

As he walked back to his truck, he pulled out his cell phone and called Toni. She didn't pick up. Figures. She was probably still mad at him. All right then, voicemail it is.

"Hi, Toni, Charles here. I've been thinking. I'm sorry, but I feel our relationship isn't going anywhere, so I think it would be best if we go our separate ways. I'm just not the right guy for you. I'm very sorry. I wish you well."

A few minutes later, he received a text message from Flora with her parents' address. He replied by asking if it was okay to visit the next day. She replied that it was.

Toni saw that Charles had left a voice mail. She dialed the number and entered her passcode. At first, what she heard angered her. But then, she realized that she was free to go out with that other man she had met.

He was tall and handsome, and seemed more her type—not all stuffy and proper, like Charles was.

The next day, Charles submitted all the paperwork regarding Flora's trailer: one copy went to her insurance company, one copy went to Franklin County, and one copy went to the city of Apalachicola. He wanted to get this done since he couldn't date anyone with an open case. With the report filed, he was free to ask Flora on a date. Around 3:30 p.m. he set out for Tallahassee, arriving at Flora's parents' house just after six. She wasn't kidding, it was a long commute, and to add to that, a nasty summer storm made the trip even longer. He was confident, though, that the insurance company would pay out about sixty days after the inspection papers were submitted. Or at least he hoped.

Carol, Flora's mother, opened the door and welcomed Charles in. Sonny, Flora's father, got up from the couch and went to shake his hand. Both of them liked this man already. He was well mannered and thoughtful. They had already heard the story from Flora, and his gesture touched them. Soon after, Victoria came into the living room and found the trunk on the living room floor. She swiftly opened the trunk door, pulled out the doll and hugged her tightly. The doll sang and as Victoria swung around the room, the doll sang and sang. Charles was touched by the joy of that child and the beauty of the child's mother. Flora came out of the kitchen. She was all made up and wearing a bright green dress which brought out her lovely emerald eyes. Her hair was pulled up, and a few curls were hanging down. He almost couldn't stand when she approached him. She whispered a soft thank you in his ear that made him shudder. The adults enjoyed the dancing and singing of Victoria and Rosie, which ended with a big hug given to Charles by Victoria. She told him he was her hero, but she didn't tell him that he was perfect for her mother. She hoped they would hit it off, so he could maybe become her new father. She really wanted a father, and he would be perfect!

After a terrific Italian dinner and before he left, Charles asked Flora if she would see him again. She accepted, and he left with a bounce in his walk. Flora's parents noticed that, and they hoped Flora had noticed it too. Sonny knew well that his wife's cooking is what did the trick!

The next day, Charles was searching for a good restaurant in Tallahassee and found that Giuseppe's had a high rating online. He called and made a reservation for Saturday evening. The restaurant was a bit pricey, but he didn't care; she was worth it. She needed some TLC, and he was going to give her some.

Flora felt like a teenager going to a prom. She had butterflies in her stomach, and her hands were trembling. She had to have her mother put makeup on her face. She put on a little black dress that she had purchased for the occasion, black kitten heels, and the pearl necklace her father had given her on her eighteenth birthday that had been his mother's. She was a vision, and when she walked out of the bedroom, Sonny thought she was a top model. He knew well that he was biased, but undoubtedly, she was the perfect woman for Charles. He prayed she was. He really wanted to see his daughter settle down, especially after how her ex had treated her. She deserved better, that was for sure.

Charles showed up with a bouquet of red roses. Flora knew well what that meant. She gave them to her mother to place in water.

"Oh my!" Carol exclaimed.

"Mom, it's not what you think," Flora said, but she knew exactly what those flowers meant. She sniffed them one more time and headed for the door.

"You look spectacular!" Charles exclaimed as he opened his truck door for her.

"Thank you, Charles. You don't look so bad yourself."

While they drove to the restaurant, Flora told Charles about Victoria's father and how he had taken off one week after she was born. Initially, her parents didn't speak to her because she got pregnant and didn't finish college. But as soon as they met Victoria their hearts melted, and they came around. Sonny had bought the trailer for their vacations, but he gave it to Flora so she could be independent. Flora eventually finished college but was unable to land a good job. So, she waited tables at the Prairies Vertes until one came along.

Charles was flabbergasted at the life she'd led and felt terribly sorry for her. But he already knew that she didn't want his pity or that of her parents. She wanted only two things: her independence and her daughter. That's all she needed.

Dinner was going wonderfully. Charles and Flora

were getting to know each other and began to realize that they were made for one another. They talked about all sorts of things and were opening up to each other. Charles had a good feeling about her; Flora likewise.

Since he was facing the door and Flora wasn't, he noticed a couple come in. It was Toni with some guy. His mood changed quickly, and his face darkened. Flora wondered what made him suddenly change that way.

"What's going on?" she asked.

"Oh, nothing, nothing—" he said but keeping his eyes on Toni. He didn't want her to meet Flora. No. He didn't want Toni to alienate this new relationship.

"Are you sure nothing's wrong?" Flora asked again.

"Absolutely," he said, but his response didn't convince her at all. She got a bit frantic and thought to call her mother. She needed some advice.

"I'm going to the ladies' room and call to see how Victoria is doing. I'll be back shortly."

He stood up and said, "Yes, of course." But he kept his eyes on Toni. The hostess led Toni and her guy to a table not too far away from Charles's table. As soon as Toni saw him, she waved at him.

Oh boy, he thought. Now what?

Flora called her mother and told her what had happened. Carol was very understanding and told her daughter that it was all right. What could possibly spoil her evening?

"Don't worry honey. It's probably nothing. Now go

back and enjoy the rest of your dinner date."

"Yes, mother." She hung up, and as she headed to her table, she noticed a beautiful brunette talking to Charles. And she wasn't just talking; she was touching him here and there in what Flora thought was an alluring way. Oh, so that's what his mood change was? He saw his old flame and *Voilà*, I'm history. Fine! She can have him! I'm out of here! She pulled out her cell phone, called a cab, and headed out the rear kitchen door. She never wanted to see this cad, again! When the cabbie picked her up, she was crying, and all her makeup was streaming down her face.

"Stupid!" she scolded herself. "What makes you think you can compete with that brunette? She's a top model or something similar, for sure!" She sniffled.

"You okay Miss?" The cabbie asked in a slight foreign accent.

"Yes, I'm fine, thank you." But she was far from fine.

When Toni finally went to sit with her date, Charles looked towards the ladies' room. He didn't see Flora. Why was she taking so long? Was Victoria ill? He waited another ten minutes. When the waitress told him that Flora had left, he asked for the check. He paid cash and left. He drove as fast as he could to her parents' house and parked across the driveway. He rushed to the door and knocked feverishly.

Sonny opened the door.

"What do you want?" Sonny asked, irritated.

Charles was puzzled. Why the attitude? What did he

do?

"I came to see Flora. Is she okay? Is Victoria okay?"

Sonny didn't let him in, even though Charles was looking over his shoulders to see if either Flora or Victoria came to the door.

"Yes, they're both fine." He said, even more irritated.

"So, what happened? Why did she leave?"

"You mean, you don't know? Flora saw you talking intimately with another woman. You two looked very close, so she left. Now, if you'll excuse me—" he said as he began closing the door.

"No, no, Sonny, I can explain." He strategically placed his foot in the doorway, to keep it open.

"I'm listening." Sonny knew that he was sincere. He could feel it. His daughter had overreacted.

"That other woman was Toni. She and I had dated, but it's over. It's been over for a while. I promise you, Sonny, I love your daughter. I loved her the moment I met her. I don't know what came over me, but I knew I just had to marry her." He stopped to take a breath. Did he just ask her hand in marriage? "Now, I know it's early, but my intentions are good, sir, I promise you!"

"Really?" Victoria yelled. "You want to marry my mom?" she asked as she ran up to her grandfather.

Sonny moved aside and let Charles come inside. Victoria ran up to Charles as he crouched down to meet her face to face.

"Yes, Victoria, I do. I only hope she will agree to

marry me."

"I know she will!" Then she turned and ran to the back of the house. "MOM!! COME OUT – NOW!"

Carol had also appeared from the kitchen, and she mused at what she heard. She went up to Charles and hugged him. "It will be fine. I promise."

"Yes, son, it will be," Sonny said as he patted Charles on the back.

They both loved Charles already, just the same as Charles loved Flora already.

Charles stared at his feet as he waited for Flora to appear. Then he saw her. His heart pounded faster when she was near. Yes, she definitely was the one.

"Flora, I'm so sorry!" He moved closer to her.

"Who was she, Charles?" she asked with a soft voice.

"Her name is Toni. She's in my past." He took both her hands. "But you – you are my future. You are the one, Flora. Please forgive me. I want to start a new life with you. What do you say?" he said as he lifted her hands to his heart and pressed them there.

Flora looked at her daughter, who was nodding yes. Then she looked at her father, who gave her a wink. Finally, she looked at her mom who had her hands crossed over her heart and was smiling from ear to ear. Then she turned to Charles and said:

"Yes, Charles, I want to start a new life with you, too, and I forgive you."

They kissed. Then Charles got down on one knee.

"I know I don't have a ring, but I wanted to propose anyway."

Flora's eyes welled.

"Flora Mantovanelli, will you marry me?"

With a lump in her throat, Flora managed to nod and say, "Yes."

#

Joanne Fisher is a Canadian-Italian-American author of her first book titled *With All of Me* and author of a short story titled *The Christmas Concert* featured in the SCWG's  anthology "Holidays." She is married to the love of her life, Dan. She lives in central Florida with Dan and her two doxies, Wally and Ozzie. Follow Joanne on Facebook @ReadJoannesBooks, on Twitter @JoannesBooks, on Instagram joannes_books_2018, or online at www.joannesbooks.com.

GRIPPING THE WAX

By Cindy Foley

The blank page stares at me. Not even a real page, like paper—the stuff you can touch. Just a blank white screen on a cold machine that can receive input through a keyboard to make words visible. Technology — amazing. Then why aren't I amazed?

I have a deadline. A publisher wants this piece on surfing Florida's beaches by next Thursday, less than a week, and I haven't even started it. When I think about the reason I moved to Florida, I want to crawl into a dark hole, pull a blanket over my head, and forget. Not that I ever can.

***

My wife and I were living in Windham, New York, a small, ski-resort town nestled deep in the Catskills. Our twin girls, five years old, were already schussing down the bunny slopes like future gold medal winners. At first, my wife resisted when I said I wanted to teach them to ski, said they were too little, they'd get hurt, but I pressed the issue. What was the point of living near the slopes if we weren't going to take advantage of them? And kids are so open and flexible at that age.

***

"You want to teach the girls to ski? Fine. You take them." She waggled a finger in my face. "You get them up in the morning, fix their breakfast, and pack their gear in the car. Make sure they're dressed warm and take them to the bathroom before they put their skis on. You can't let them go in the bathroom by themselves. You have to go with them. How are you going to do that?"

***

"Aren't you coming with us?" Shocked, I retorted with how much time I spent with her and the girls even when I didn't want to. I didn't mean it the way it sounded. I should have kept my big mouth shut. Hindsight was 20/20.

***

"Are you saying you don't like to be with us?"

"I didn't say that." Was she PMS-ing or something? The "or something" was more like it, but I didn't catch on to what it was right then.

I took the girls, and my older niece to help with the restroom department and taught them all how to ski.

***

That spring, we were planning our annual spring break trip to visit my grandfather in Eau Gallie, Florida. My wife and I had been taking this trip since we'd been in grad school together, since before the girls were born.

"See, it's only a quarter inch from the ocean." I tapped the map I was showing the girls.

They clapped with glee. "Can we collect shells? Can we swim in Poppy's pool? Are we going to Disney World?" They had a hundred questions.

"You two go play. Mommy and I have to finish planning."

After they left the room, I reached for my wife's hand, but she pulled it away.

"I won't be going."

I stared at her. "You're kidding."

She wouldn't meet my eyes. "No, I'm not. I need a break."

"You need a break?" My brain went on high alert.

"Yes." She glared straight into my eyes. I was stunned by the vehemence in them. "I work my tail off around here. You don't lift a hand with the girls. I have a full-time job and work just as hard as you. Besides that, I do all the cleaning, the grocery shopping, and the cooking, and the laundry, and manage our finances..." Her voice drifted off as if she were going to cry, but she didn't. Instead, she bit her lip and crossed her arms in her 'I'm angry' stance.

"I help with the girls." I tried to ease the tension. "I scrub my skid marks in the toilet too." I smiled and winked at her.

"And leave the toothpaste cap off, and don't rinse the sink after you shave. When it comes to the girls, all you do is play with them. I'm always the bad guy."

I put my arms around her, but she pushed me away.

"Don't try schmoozing me," she said.

Her bitching was really pissing me off. Scared the girls half the time. Somebody had to be their buffer.

"You don't do everything." I went into full offense mode. "I do most of my own laundry, and I do the yard work." The hairs on the back of my neck prickled. "What the fuck's going on?"

"Don't you dare use that tone with me. Are you even listening? I do everything around here, and what thanks do I get from you. I'm tired of it. Go on. You see what it's like to be both the mom and the dad for once."

***

She didn't change her mind and over the next week kept a cool distance. I went to Florida without her. I hoped the time apart would do us both good. Maybe it was true that every couple needed a break once in a while. I swallowed my disbelief.

***

Spring break in Florida is crazy fun. The weather couldn't have been better. Canova Beach was an excellent place for picking shells. 7-11 Slurpees were the best coolant after a sweltering day in the sun and salt spray. Disney wore us out. Nightly swims in Poppy's pool and his great cooking made for a perfect end to perfect days. The week passed by way too fast.

I did a lot of thinking on that trip. My wife and I had both made our choices. She'd always said she wasn't letting marriage and family get in the way of her career. I'd been cool with that. We'd known it was going to be difficult when we decided to have kids. Twins came as a surprise and made things harder. We'd both been riding a rough surf, hadn't we? But, now that the girls were a little older and starting to take care of themselves, I thought things seemed a bit easier.

Busy with my demanding job, maybe I hadn't been paying close enough attention. I'd help out more when the girls and I got back.

I missed my wife, and, by the end of our vacation, I was ready to go home. I'd managed breakfast before the second sip of morning coffee, wet towels and bathing suits, sandy feet, dishes, baths, and checkers with Poppy. The last night there, I even watched the movie *What Women Want* starring Mel Gibson and Helen Hunt. I had a new perspective.

***

When we returned to Windham, my wife slathered the girls with kisses and hugs. "Did you have a good time? You're peeling. Didn't Daddy make you wear sunscreen? I missed you."

She gave me the cold shoulder.

Warning, warning. Danger—Will Robinson.

That evening, after she insisted on putting the girls to bed even though I said I would, she came into the den. She was crying. I immediately went to her side. "What's wrong, baby?"

"Don't touch me," she said. "I have to tell you something." She sobbed into her hands.

I put my arm around her shoulder. She shrugged it off.

I backed away and clenched my fists behind my back. A knot restricted my throat. "What do you have to tell me?"

She glared at me, her face pinched with anger, her eyes swollen and red. "This is all your fault. If you'd been more attentive, if you'd showed you cared, that you thought about me ..."

"What's going on?" My heart pounded in my chest. "Jesus-H-Christ, I just got home. You meet me at the door like I got leprosy or something, and now you're blaming me. For what?" My blood boiled. Her next statement slammed into me like a freight train.

"I'm seeing someone else."

I fell into the closest chair I could find. If she'd said she wanted a divorce, I'd have probably wondered if she was having an affair. But her point blank confession left me speechless. A heavy weight settled onto my chest.

"Aren't you going to say something?"

My brain wouldn't function. "I'll sleep on the couch."

***

We went on like that for a month. I wondered if the girls asked why Daddy wasn't there when they ran into our bedroom on the weekends. They didn't giggle as much in the paralyzing tension that crackled throughout the house. I didn't ask my wife where she was going when she went out, nor could I go back to our bed even though, after the first week, she asked me to and begged me to forgive her. Forgiving wasn't the hardest part. Forgetting was impossible. I talked to no one about our problem. Instead, I clung to it, let it eat at my gut and worm its way through my numb brain.

**

My mother asked me if I was on a diet.

"You look skinny,' she said. "You work too hard. You looked so nice and tan when you got back from Florida. Much as I hate to say it, maybe you ought to go back, take the whole family this time. Give up that stressful job. Live a little." She squinted and leaned in closer to my face like she always did when she was trying to see inside my head. She knew something was up and had the good grace not to ask what it was.

I had no idea what was going to bring this to a head or how my wife and I were going to resolve it. Life stalled like an engine out of gas. Interaction with her was dead calm, as suffocating as still air before a storm, an avalanche after the fall.

**

It was a muggy night when a gunshot woke me from a restless sleep on the sticky leather couch. Immediately awake, I bounded up the stairs. The girls were running down the hall toward the master bedroom. I'd never seen that door shut. I caught them and gave them a quick hug.

"Come on, back to bed. Everything is fine." I carried them to their room, plopped them on the bed, and gave them both a good tickling. "You're fine. I'm going to check on Mommy." I gave them my sternest look. "Stay here, understand?"

Their eyes were glassy and wide. They nodded.

I left them huddled together and ran down the hall.

The master suite was locked. I knocked once and softly called my wife's name. When I didn't get an answer, I grabbed the key from atop the door frame and unlocked the door.

***

The horror remains with me to this day, the blood spatter and chunks of whatever on the ceiling and wall, my wife sprawled on the floor, a crimson pool spreading under what was left of her head, an acrid mix of gunpowder and iron, the gun—my gun, the closet door ajar, the safe where we kept our important stuff— open. I couldn't help it. I threw up.

After weeks of idling in a blank stupor, my brain chose then to kick in. I backed out of the bedroom, closed the door, and hurried down the hall.

"It's okay." I hugged the girls. "Everything's going to be okay."

"What was that noise, Daddy?"

"Probably a car backfiring outside."

Of course, they had to ask, "Where's Mommy?"

"She must have gone to the store. Get under the covers."

"Stay with us, Daddy." I waited until they fell asleep to call the cops.

***

Later, after the coroner, after the EMT's, after a thousand questions, I wondered if I would ever tell the girls the truth of what really happened, and even if I did, could I ever tell them why?

It took me decades to figure out there were no answers, that it didn't help to keep asking. Sometimes all you could do was ride the wave.

***

I sold the house and most of our things, packed the girls and their stuffed animals into my car, and moved to Florida. The attraction of a balmy southern paradise soon gave way to oppressive heat, a threat of dangerous hurricanes, and a painful sense of loss whenever I thought of what I'd left behind. No matter how much I wanted to, I couldn't go back. I didn't have time for a pity party. I had the girls to raise.

***

Life has a funny way of throwing curve balls. If I'd never gone on that spring break vacation, I'd have never seen my girls become Olympic swimmers. Instead of a powerhouse career and climbing corporate ladders, I grew my hair past my shoulders, learned how to build surfboards, and became a published author.

I like me better these days.

Florida's got its good and its bad, beaches and sand spurs, lots of sun and voracious mosquitoes. It's not the mountains, but then —surfing is kind of like skiing.

***

One day, after my girls are settled, and their children are saying that gramps is losing something he never had, I hope I'm still riding the waves and writing stories. I'd much rather deal with the sharks than the dark demons that lurk just beneath the surface when my feet are gripping the wax.

#

Cindy Foley is the author of *The Truth Lies...a Florida Saga*, winner of the 2016 SCWG Don Argo award for Florida literature, author of the young adult novel *I, Clawed: The Renewal*, and the  poetry chapbook *Water Drops*. She contributed to the Space Coast Writers' Guild anthologies *Gratitude*, *Spring*, *Friends*, *Perseverance*, and *Holidays*. Cindy is president of the Space Coast Writers Guild and an organizing Director of the Brevard Authors Society. Visit her online at www.cindyafoley.com or email her at cindyfoley123@gmail.com.

THE PARALEGAL

By Terri Friedlander

Darcia Solano did not move to Miami to find herself a wealthy husband as her family suspected. Her mother's dire warnings about ravaging hurricanes and rampant drug deals sounded as though the woman had watched entirely too much *Miami Vice* on television. Darcia proudly considered herself a "yuppie," a young urban professional, focused and determined to set the legal world on fire. Well, if not the world, at least her modern, clean, adopted city of Miami, which she called the Manhattan of the South. At twenty-four years old, her plans had been happening right on schedule. Sure, she answered an occasional personal ad and dated a few halfway decent men, but marriage was nowhere near the top of her to-do list.

She only craved one lucky break to catapult her to the big leagues of the legal world. To be hired at a white-shoe law firm located in a gleaming marble building on Brickell Avenue that specialized in mergers and acquisitions. She never imagined she would be kept waiting almost two hours for the job interview.

Lawyers!

That afternoon, bubbling with anticipation, Darcia arrived twenty minutes early in a rainy downpour for the four-thirty interview. As the minutes ticked by like an eternity, visitors came and left while she sat there, squirming, glancing at the wall clock, practically memorizing every page of the *Time* magazine which featured Anita Hill's shocking testimony against Clarence Thomas. At six o'clock Darcia tossed the issue so hard against the table that a nearby bowl of mints bounced into the air, almost crashing to the floor. She spotted the reflection of her teased blonde bangs and blue tailored suit with its brass buttons in the high-gloss wood. *Be patient*, she told herself and took a deep breath.

Fifteen minutes later, a pencil-thin woman in a silky low-cut blouse and tight gray skirt finally appeared. "I'm Heather, Mr. Ritti's secretary. He will see you now. Please follow me."

Trailing Heather down the hall, Darcia forgot her speech about being the most competent paralegal in Miami. *Even if he offers me a ten thousand dollar increase, I'd be insane to work for anyone so inconsiderate.*

When she entered the office, Giuseppe Ritti stood like a perfect gentleman, extended his hand and motioned for her to sit. She caught his eye searching her ring finger as though checking for a wedding band. *Nope, not married*, she thought about saying but instead forced a smile through the awkward silence.

"Forgive me for keeping you waiting," he began. "Would you like a café or water or a can of soda?"

"No, thanks. I'm fine." Clearing her throat, she sat back and handed him her resume. Several litigation boxes sat in one corner of the office with a white leather couch in the other. Pink message slips, yellow legal pads, and an inbox piled with newspapers, memos and envelopes cluttered the mahogany desk. Outside the tall windows, the rain had stopped, and the setting sun gleamed off the blue waters of Biscayne Bay as million dollar yachts and cruise ships dotted the horizon. A bulky computer monitor with the letters IBM on the front sat near a Rolodex of business cards by his phone opposite a can of seltzer and a bag of crumbled potato chips.

Having researched him in *The American Lawyer*, Darcia knew that forty-two-year-old Giuseppe Ritti had graduated Harvard, started practicing law in Connecticut and had relocated to Miami five years earlier. Missing from his profile was his refined style that also reeked of arrogance ... and money. His starched French-cuff white shirt featured his initials engraved in blue thread above the heavy gold cufflinks. He wore a solid gray textured wool suit with a red and blue Hermes silk tie. The custom shirt, exquisite tie, tailored suit. His black hair was perfectly coiffed against his olive skin. Everything about the man screamed power.

"My conference call lasted longer than expected." He studied her resume and picked up the seltzer to take a gulp. "Now please tell me about yourself."

Darcia proceeded to talk about her internship and the cases she'd been given. After boasting about her legal and technical skills and how she could speak and translate Spanish fluently, she hoped he'd be sufficiently impressed. In Miami, with its strong Latin American and Cuban connections, her bilingual skills had already become an asset as valuable as gold.

The partner grilled her with questions about her degree and prior experience with litigation and corporate law. Darcia thought she responded brilliantly to each one.

Suddenly, Giuseppe Ritti smiled and leaned towards her with a twinkle in his eye.

"Now that I know what you do professionally, what do you like to do socially?"

"Excuse me?" Darcia lurched back so fast that she knocked the purse off the chair. *Is this guy really flirting with me? In an interview?* Feeling a pit in her stomach, she noticed his eyes gazing at her chest. "I, uh... like to get together with friends for dinner."

"I like to get together with friends too... in a hot tub." Then he laughed.

Darcia practically choked and inhaled slowly. *He did not just say hot tub? Ewe!*

Out of the blue, Ritti grabbed a sheet of paper and scribbled an offer for her to start the following week at fifteen thousand a year more than her current salary.

"Welcome to McGovern and Knight."

***

On her first day, Darcia had chosen to wear an Ann Taylor gray herringbone suit with a high-collared crème blouse and Life Strides black pumps, hoping her desired look screamed yuppie. Strutting into the lobby wearing strappy stilettos, Heather White was draped in a sleeveless red dress with a plunging neckline that hugged every curve. *Dress for the job you want to have,*

Darcia smirked as she followed the impossible six-inch heels.

After completing multiple employment forms and spending the afternoon with two new attorneys in the training room, Darcia jotted notes on the intricate litigation systems. Heather gave her a rushed tour of the library and word processing center and led her to a small cubicle bearing her name near the copy center.

I have arrived, she smiled, logged onto her IBM computer and got to work.

By Friday, Darcia had seen and spoken more to Heather than Giuseppe Ritti. Most of the casework was moved around the office in sealed interoffice mail envelopes or in person by Heather White.

"You sure know your way around. How long have you worked here?" she asked Heather, who had unexpectedly sat in the spare chair beside the desk.

"Only four months. This place is always nonstop busy. Every day I learn something new."

"And what do you make of Giuseppe Ritti? Is he the biggest rainmaker in the firm?"

"I think so. He bills out twelve hour days and most weekends. With his mountain of billable hours, he doesn't mind paying overtime. Working for him is amazing, but sometimes I feel like I don't have a life anymore."

"I heard that could happen," Darcia said, adjusting the height of her new leather armchair. "And I'll bet they expect sacrifices from the few women they hire. I'm sure I caught him checking my ring finger as though I wouldn't have been considered for this job if I was married or engaged."

"I doubt that he would do anything like that," Heather said unconvincingly.

"You sound like you're defending the guy," Darcia exclaimed. "Ritti went a little too far on my interview when he told me he likes hot tubbing with friends. And last week when he saw me working late, he offered to take me to dinner at the Biltmore Hotel ... like he's really thinking about food!"

"Are you sure you heard him correctly?" Heather shrugged. "He has a brilliant mind, and he's a workaholic, like all the Ivy Leaguers here. Don't take anything Mr. Ritti says personally."

"What do you mean?"

"Have you ever seen a rodeo? When that man is under pressure, he becomes an attacking bull, berating associates and almost bringing them to tears."

"Has he ever said anything inappropriate to you?" Darcia probed cautiously.

"Well, once I wore an ankle-length dress, and he said I had great legs so why would I hide them? I shrugged it off as a backhanded compliment. But at the end of the day, he told me not to wear that 'frumpy' outfit again because he didn't want a legal secretary who dressed like a nun. I just don't let it get to me."

"That's insane! Did you report him?" Darcia felt the need to apologize for misjudging the woman by her high heels and pretty face.

"To whom? ... Nah. I need this job. Anyways, wherever I go, it would be the same nonsense. Sort of goes with the territory in this city. Take a look outside. The streets of Miami are packed with stunning girls who dress like Ford models. In a minute, he'd replace me with someone younger, hotter, and smarter. Besides, Giuseppe's all talk, but he is basically harmless."

"The hypocrisy of these high-priced lawyers who write sexual harassment laws for a living is ridiculous," Darcia said bleakly.

"Listen to me. You'll do fine around here if you shrug it off and keep your mouth shut."

***

Two weeks went by without incident. Darcia loved the work she did. And, like Heather, she arrived earlier and stayed well past nine o'clock every evening without being asked. Quickly she had memorized every partner's name and most of the associates. They kept her busy filing briefs, researching precedents, and proofing contracts.

Then one day she walked past Heather's desk and found her trembling with tears in her eyes. Darcia had come to admire the woman's confidence and composure and understood why she made excuses for him. From his office, he glared in Heather's direction and continued shouting as though not noticing Darcia outside.

"Am I going to have to take you over my knee and

spank you the next time you don't use your brains, imbecile?"

As her blood pumped so hard in her veins, Darcia thought she might burst an artery. Instead of rushing to rescue her only friend in the office, she remembered Heather's own words about keeping her mouth shut. *He has the gall to humiliate an employee and threaten to spank her?*

Two associates walked by within earshot of the brazen scolding that sounded abusive, plain and simple. They exchanged a look and hastened their pace, diverting their glance.

A few minutes later, Heather dashed into the ladies room and Darcia followed.

"Are you okay? This is outrageous," Darcia yelled. "Ritti crosses the line again like he's The Godfather or something. What's worse is how the other lawyers continue looking the other way."

"Yeah. What a jerk, huh?"

"Has he ever talked about spanking you before? This is outright sexual harassment. The guy's a pig."

"So what should I do about it? If I lose my job, will it change anything?"

"Quit! And run, don't walk, to any law firm in this big city and file a lawsuit against his nasty ass!"

"I can't."

"Why not? If we gather some witnesses, we can prove that the partners knew about Ritti's obnoxious behavior and you'd win the lottery. Businesses have a legal obligation to provide employees with a safe work environment ... there's nothing safe about this guy. He's brutal to women and deserves to be put in his place. Or better yet, be fired."

"Ha! Don't kid yourself. Ritti brings in more money than all the partners. He won't be fired. Never! Maybe they'd slap his hand, but that's even a long shot. He's a rainmaker. You and me, we're dispensable."

"Trust me. Start documenting every word. Date, time, and exact whisper. Every innuendo and insensitive remark that comes out of this fat pig's mouth. We can't let this continue. How about we get dinner tonight in the Art Deco District and formulate our battle plan?"

As though she was on a mission, Darcia began secretly researching harassment cases in the workplace. When someone appeared, she'd exit the search program and return to her casework. The more she read, the more confident she became that Ritti could be taken down and she could be the one to do it. She just needed to convince Heather at dinner that evening that it was worth the risk.

"How long have you lived in Miami?" Heather asked once they were seated at her favorite people watching spot, Joe's Stone Crab.

"Five years. I won a scholarship to Florida International University, left Trenton, New Jersey after high school graduation, steered my 1992 Pontiac Firebird south and the rest is history. No more winter blizzards or year-round filthy air pollution. I love it here. Where are you from?"

"Chicago. Hated the windy city and finally got up the courage to move last year. But life here is not what I expected. I'm always working and never get to the beach. I thought living in Miami Beach would feel like a permanent vacation."

"Me too," Darcia agreed ruefully. "I hungered for the endless summers, palm trees, and sandy beaches. When I graduated FIU magna cum laude and secured an internship in the Miami-Dade District Attorney's office, I clocked twelve hour days in the hopes of securing an entry-level job offer. I've been climbing the legal ladder ever since. And I never met anyone as blatantly off the charts and disrespectful to women as Giuseppe Ritti! Let's do something to at least frighten this guy's dapper ass."

***

The following day, Darcia didn't notice him lurking at the lobby elevator bank until she pressed the button. He turned to ogle her and their eyes locked. *Am I going to be trapped alone with this pervert all the way to the thirty-ninth floor? But maybe everything happens for a reason.*

"I like your turtleneck sweater, blondie," Ritti smirked as the doors closed.

How I wish I had a tape recorder right now. And he has the nerve to call me blondie? "Thank you."

"But I really like your low-cut ones much better. Are

you wearing a black bra today?"

Darcia's cheeks felt hotter than fire. *If he touches me, all bets are off.*

He leaned towards her, eyes on her chest with one hand reaching for a breast when the doors opened. Instantly, she bolted for her desk, feeling nauseous, and made another mental entry in the secret notebook she had named the 'sleazy journal.' *Blondie!*

Later that same day, she returned from lunch to find an urgent message to get to Ritti's office immediately. When she arrived, his face appeared as red as a tamale and rage saturated his beady eyes.

"Are these your initials? DS? Did you proofread this document on the wrongful termination case against Academy Software?"

"Yes, sir."

"Well, well. I guess D.S. must mean Dumb Shit! Didn't you check that the plaintiff is suing our client for $300,000, not $30,000? Your little mistake could have cost the firm thousands of dollars, dumb shit!"

Ritti pointed to a paragraph on the second page and sure enough. Darcia had missed it. "I'm sorry, sir. It won't happen again."

"You can bet that if you make another mistake like this, your pretty little ass will be out of here so fast you won't ever work for another firm within a hundred miles of here. Am I making myself clear?"

"Yes. Crystal clear, sir."

Darcia swallowed hard and practically ran from the office, trying to stay composed until reaching her cubicle. A little while later, Heather appeared, shaking, looking as though her beloved cat just died.

"I just caught Ritti rifling through my desk drawer for no reason," Heather said breathlessly. "Imagine if he found the journal and the notes I've been keeping on him ... I know you want documentation about his bad behavior and innuendos, but I can't do it, Darcia. There's no chance of beating him. Besides, I never wanted a big settlement. In a public hearing, he'd retaliate and attack me like a pit bull, dice me into little pieces and embarrass me to death. Sorry, but if you insist on going after him, you're on your own."

"Your timing is impeccable. This morning he calls me 'blondie' and almost gropes me in the elevator! And now he says I'm a dumb shit and threatens to fire me. If the firm terminates me because of my mistakes, which now stands at one, by the way, the whole thing is over. Without you and the others testifying with me, we'd have no chance against the almighty Giuseppe Ritti or this seedy firm. Don't you see? We can only force change by sticking together."

"I'm sorry. I can't. I need this job. I'm out." Heather turned and dashed to her desk, heels clicking.

Darcia shuddered. She'd go it alone if she had to. *'Threats of spankings. Gropings. Black bra. Dumb shit. Hot tubs.'* Giuseppe Ritti must be stopped. If only she could discover another tidbit before filing a harassment case against his crude ass. *But will they believe him or me?*

In the meantime, Heather stopped returning Darcia's calls and invitations to lunch. Then, that week, the usually tense atmosphere on their floor waned relaxed and peaceful as Ritti seemed to have disappeared. The entire litigation department quietly slipped out at five-thirty without its tormentor.

Rumors circulated that he'd taken his wife on a Royal Caribbean cruise vacation for their wedding anniversary. *The leech who acted as God's gift to women was married! Surprise, surprise.*

Seizing the opportunity to loosen lips, Darcia approached a male attorney whom she had recently worked with on a merger. "Hey, Ricardo. You busy tonight? Let's head down to Lincoln Road for happy hour. I found this Latin place that makes authentic tapas. Spread the word."

One by one, her coworkers arrived and joined her at the bar while Madonna's Vogue blasted from the speakers on the dance floor.

"Can you believe how calm the firm is without Ritti around?" she asked Ricardo casually after ordering a second glass of wine.

"That guy is wound tighter than his twenty-thousand dollar Rolex."

Darcia laughed as she looked at the Timex on her wrist. "I heard he likes relaxing in a hot tub with his closest buddies. Did he ever invite you to the party?"

"No way! But one of his former secretaries told me

that he invited her to those hot tub events all the time. Britney was hotter than a bikini model, and Ritti drooled over her cleavage like a dog out in the Florida humidity. Gossip has it that she vanished after complaining about him 'groping' her in the conference room one evening."

Someone else claimed that a female associate quit a few days after Ritti threatened to 'spank her' for making some kind of mistake. "I'd bet my life that she scorned his hot tub invites too and got the boot."

As the wine flowed, the entertaining gossip became juicier. Darcia did not doubt that it was true even though some stories sounded like they came from *The National Enquirer,* not a typical day in a big law firm.

But the juicy hearsay wouldn't hold up in court without sworn testimony from the victims themselves. Somehow, she needed to contact each one personally. Then she remembered his Rolodex of names and business cards perched like a permanent fixture on his desk. She would bet every one of those phone numbers was stored there.

At five o'clock the next morning, Darcia arrived bright and early at her cubicle and tiptoed to Heather's top desk drawer for the spare key to Ritti's office.

After turning the key in the door and opening it, she reached for the lights. Stretched out on the couch, naked as a newborn, lay Giuseppe Ritti with a male associate kneeling before him in a most compromising position.

Giuseppe turned and looked into her eyes. "So Blondie, you finally decided to join the party!"

Darcia turned and bolted from the office, grabbed her purse and never looked back.

***

A year later, the trial of Darcia Solano versus McGovern and Knight hit the courts as well as the front page of the *Miami Herald* and every other newspaper. With Heather White's bulletproof testimony, along with sworn statements from dozens of other female and male employees, they convinced the jury that the firm's partners knew of Ritti's boorish behavior but ignored it. The judge awarded a hefty verdict in Solano's favor. The once mighty and unbeatable Giuseppe Ritti resigned in disgrace. With their generous settlement, both women graduated from the University Of Miami School of Law and put their names in a new lobby, vowing never to keep a client waiting.

Twenty years later, Harvey Weinstein and Matt Lauer didn't see the law firm of Solano and White barreling in their direction.

# # #

Terri Friedlander is a native New Yorker. She has held numerous jobs, including writer, college professor, teacher, freelance journalist, and MIS Director of an international law firm. Terri is the author of  *Work Hard Play Hard*, *Chasing Her Destiny*, and *The Dorm*. She also created the newspaper column *In Front of the Classroom*. Loving life in Florida, she can be reached online at www.terrifriedlander.com.

MOM'S APPROVAL

By Michael Gabriel

They exited the terminal into the distressing July heat, the air liquid and possessed with a weight that allowed only shallow breaths and small movements. Mark shepherded the group across to the rental car, each grappling with luggage and the vertiginous sense of displacement, fatigue, and loss in his own way. The result was an odd mixture of melancholy and merriment fed by caffeine and alcohol.

The sprawling hotel high-rise was set hard against the Intracoastal Waterway adjacent to the causeway, a marina skirting its base as a grudging concession to the locale. They navigated the winding concrete pathways arching over impossibly blue water and suffered the cacophonous result of piped-in music and the din of the kiddie pool. After checking in, the exhausted family members consulted each other and their respective spouses and agreed to meet in a couple of hours, planning, variously, to nap, eat, or drink. An eight-foot Tyvek banner in the lobby announced "Welcome Bodybuilders" and served only to enhance their loss of equilibrium. Their chartered boat would leave at three.

Only four days prior, Mark had picked up the phone with the breathless confusion that is the consequence of a 3:00 a.m. call, garnering no solace from its inevitability. The unfailing accuracy of her diagnosis resulted, that night, in tears of loss and the guilt of the living tinged with relief. Solid, restful sleep had been impossible in the days subsequent. Although her practical nature had ordered the final details long ago, the only remaining task was a coordination of the siblings' travel plans, Mark filled his days with a flurry of calls to his mother's husband, the funeral home, and *Poseidon's Reach*. She'd chosen the cremation and service at sea as a natural end to her life's love of the water and as a desire to unburden the family. An amorphous resistance that Mark attributed to grief dominated the conversations with her husband William as he acquiesced to Mark coordinating the details.

Now gratefully alone as his wife napped, Mark wandered the meeting rooms and grounds marveling at the mesomorphic patrons. On display were a kaleidoscope of bulging body sizes sheathed in a taut mandarin skin tint with arms akimbo and topped with helmeted, perfectly coiffed do's. Oils and lotions were in constant use, and the aggregate smell was overwhelming. Their endless preening and flexing doubled as they paused before any mirrored surface to admire and judge. He was invisible.

Mark repaired to the poolside bar, sidled up to his closest brother, and squinted at the precariously placed television stuffed into the overhead thatch, its display trumpeting the approaching daily afternoon torrential event. They spoke sparingly and exchanged more in silence than in conversation, fascinated at the carnival reel spinning by. Each had enjoyed the flexibility of monthly visits since mom's diagnosis five years ago and, as such, fell more easily into the tropical setting and each other's' company than their siblings did. Within the hour, as if by design, their two other brothers and sister settled around, and the family traded remembrances, laughter, and barbs buoyed by their shared strength.

Mom would have approved.

The breeze increased, and the searing heat thinned the poolside population as the air crackled with rustled palm fronds and distant thunder. Their spouses filtered in easily, joining the revelry, the busy bartender grateful for the unexpected mid-afternoon pop. Conversation continued, rising in volume and wrapped in the solid feel until Mark consulted his watch and called for the check. "We should head over," he said as he dropped more than he needed to on the bar. Someone accounted the flurry of bills as a gust of wind forced a chair skittering across the concrete decking, the hollow aluminum legs keening its warning.

Mark's conversations with *Poseidon's Reach* had been frustrating. The service had claimed initially that no boat was available over this weekend and citing a postponement of ten days. They'd reluctantly succumbed to Mark's undeniable logic concerning available charter boats in South Florida, acquiescing to the family's need for a timely closure. The "bereavement consultant" he'd dealt with was named Ingram Fergusson, a gentleman who spoke with an exaggerated diction, his manner a cultivated balance of obsequious pretention.

The group made their way along the crisscross patchwork of docks, looking for the pier and slip number Mark had been given, as the blinding sun drove the temperatures higher on a gusty wind. As the family neared the end of the longest pier, they were met by a tall, pot-bellied man garbed incongruously in a midnight blue jumpsuit and flanked by two younger men. The tall man's eyes darted among the approaching males and, at random, offered his hand, beginning "Mr..?" Mark thrust his hand out, interrupting, "Yeah, I'm Mark."

"Ingram Fergusson" was the man's unnecessary response; he enunciated each syllable of his name as though he wished there were more. Closer now, Mark noticed the perfection of his comb-over, despite the wind, his blotched, mottled skin and the stitched logo of *Poseidon's Reach* at the breast pocket of his immaculately pressed uniform. Mark suddenly felt the need to wash his hands.

The young men were introduced as the crew of the thirty-seven foot Bertram that sat bobbing gently in the slip; their handshakes seemed tentative, their eyes never met solidly with any of the group. A few of the family dropped gingerly over the transom as Ingram intoned, "So we're all here?" glancing at his watch.

"No, we're waiting for the, uh, husband of the, uh, deceased." Mark stumbled at both references uncomfortable with any other. Slowly, attention shifted to the rear deck of the Bertram as each became aware. Sitting on a draped table that was bolted to the deck was a plain black box no more than six inches on a side and eight inches high; the realization of what it held sobered the group and brought tears to more than one. Conversations became muted and time passed with anxious looks at both the approaching storms and the parking lot.

Mark's concern creased his brow and pushed him back up the pier to call his mother's number, knowing that no answer, considering the one hour travel time, was preferable. The electronic ring in his ear was interrupted by a woman's reedy, quavering, "Wilson residence." The shock of an answer and her gender had Mark stumbling over words. She identified herself as William's nurse and delivered the news that his doctor had confined him to bed. "He's in mourning," came the pronouncement as she gently lowered the receiver. He remembered those words having been spoken several times over the last few days and, until now, had thought of them as the man's obtuse request for assistance in this weekend's preparation. As a result, Mark had dropped the thinly veiled animosity they'd shared over the years, in deference to her, and soldiered on with the planning. Now, the pieces fell together and a dull throb he'd carried behind his eyes all day pulsed into a pain that wobbled his knees as he steadied himself against the creosote-soaked rail. The air he sucked in deep breaths on the way back to the boat brought to mind the heat and insistence of a hairdryer.

Gathered in the overcooled cabin of the Bertram, the family's expectant looks turned to incredulity at the stunning turn. Their conversation revealed, through a flurry of emotion and hot words, a consensus to shove off and complete the ceremony, the urgency born of a desire to end the ordeal and of the darkening skies to the west. They returned to the sun-splashed fiberglass deck, relayed the decision to Ingram, and settled into the available seating, their consternation palpable. Still on the pier, the funereal presence rubbed his papery hands together, making no move to board, saying, "Of course. There's just the matter of payment." The jolt that pierced the group was electric, the confusion complete. After a moment of cross-talk, he added, "You, sir, are the only one with whom I spoke," his pretentious diction particularly grating and directed pointedly at Mark. The apparent "prearrangement" they all assumed existed, didn't.

This time, their conference was short; they would grant their mothers' final wish on their own, without the implied benefit of *Poseidon's Reach*. Each retreated over the transom with their feelings evolving to anger and determination. Mark scooped the box containing his mother's earthly remains, set it on his hip and muttered a curt farewell to Mr. Fergusson as he strode away. A moment later, as Ingram's eyes fell to the now empty table on board, the smug façade crumbled and he lurched towards Mark, "Hey, you can't..." The four brothers came together instantly, shoulder to shoulder and walled access to the object of Ingram's grasp. Mark snapped around abruptly, "We're taking this with us!" he spat, jabbing a trembling finger at Ingram's blanched face and fighting hot tears behind his sunglasses.

Walking back to the hotel was a blurred journey on wobbly legs escorted within the cocoon of family. The towering storms cast a shadow over the pool area, and the deck chairs once again held the cartoonish excess of the musclebound who were swilling gallons of purified water and sports drinks, oblivious to all but the uniformity of their coloring.

Back in the hotel room, Mark set the box of ashes next to the TV that was bolted to the dresser and fell into a swivel chair as someone thrust a beer into his tremulous hand. The post-adrenalin rush spawned conversation that was at once boastful and trepidatious; they were unclear as to their legal standing about their possession of the ashes. No clear plan emerged from the tumult and Mark cast around for an answer. Opinions flowed freely from the more assertive and only muddied their options; emotions began to run as Mark allowed the current to find its depth. He turned towards his closest brother, quiet as is his way, and prodded him,

"What do you think?" Jack looked up slowly.

"How far is the beach?" he said simply, his dark eyes flashing around the crowded room.

"End of the causeway, can't be a five-minute drive."

And that's all there was. They were on the sand in ten minutes, moving barefoot across the deserted stretch of a normally crowded beach. Mark tossed a nervous look to the west and saw: nothing. The threatening squall line had simply dissipated, leaving a benign stack of shrinking cumulous and feathery wisps in front of the brilliant tangerine glow of the setting sun. The ocean was glass, with the foamed edge of the incoming tide gently lapping at the granite smooth, wet sand.

They came together without direction and formed a circle, their arms draped easily over one another's shoulder. Each spoke, or didn't, comfortable in the others' choice. Wading into the silky, warm tide, Mark opened the box and tipped the contents, the finality of it burst a cathartic dam and caused a shameless sobbing that shook him deeply. There was a breathtaking symmetry in the swirling ashes intermingling with the brilliant color of the proffered flowers floating gently in the crystalline saltwater and seen through the blurred vision they shared as one. Drifting apart, they found solace in the private words each spoke only to her, knowing once again the comfort of her smile and touch.

Mom would have approved.

# # #

Michael Gabriel is a retired airline pilot who has spent over forty years in the industry. He has written *The Force Of Destiny*, a biography of his father, Colonel Arnald D. Gabriel. It is the story of a  promising high school musician whose life was interrupted by a world war and his eventual rise to the pinnacle of his profession as the Commander and Conductor of the Air Force Band. Michael and his wife Trish live in Vero Beach, Florida.

A Snow Bird's View of Florida

By Barbara Hanson

A pod of dolphins, shiny and smooth
breaking the surface of the lagoon.

A determined goose leading her goslings
in a single line
across a parking lot.

A scoop of pelicans
landing in shallow water
in search of lunch.

A herd of manatees
huddling together in a canal
during a cold spell.

Screeching wild parrots
leaving a bright green blur in the sky.

Elegant sandhill cranes,
white egrets, wading ibises,
flamboyant flamingos,
ancient turtles
basking in the sun.
Tropical flora

bougainvillea, oleander, poinciana,
multi-colored hibiscus,
plumeria, magnolias, gardenias,
Florida irises.

Majestic palms, crape myrtle, swamp dogwood,
red bottlebrush trees,
each with a special allure.

A warm breezy sunbath
on the patio
perfect for thought and meditation.

A leisurely stroll
through Turtle Creek Sanctuary
a new view of nature
at each turn in the path.

A hair-raising ride on a zip line
above exotic animals, birds,
plant life.

A viewing of Highwaymen art,
enjoying the unique textile exhibit at
the Ruth Funk Center.

Being thoroughly entertained
at first-class playhouses
along the east coast.

Spending blissful hours
discovering unusual treasures
in the myriads of antique shops.

Being enthralled by botanical gardens
Leu, Fairchild, McKee, Bok Tower.

Appreciating art walks, flea markets
concerts, craft beers,
happy hours on outside patios,
exciting missile launches,
writing groups, art classes.

The tactile pleasure of beach sand,
warm and comforting
under bare feet.

Dunes, sea oats, shells of every hue,
wave-polished seaglass
darting little sand pipers
sand crabs scampering in the surf,
tiny toddlers giggling
while building castles.

The aroma of sunscreen
mixed with periodic whiffs
of water-borne seaweed.

Brightly painted toenails
protruding from flip flops,
flowing dresses, shorts, bikinis.

Flaming sunsets, pink sunrises,
brief afternoon showers and
occasional torrential rain
dousing the landscape.

Fresh, succulent seafood,
pecan-encrusted grouper,
chocolate-covered potato chips,
real key lime pie,
authentic Mexican cuisine
Warm, friendly greetings at church,
at the grocery store,
at the bakery,
in the neighborhood.

A snow "Bird of Paradise."

# # #

Barbara Hanson, M.A., M.S., co-authored
the book *Vermont: Wilderness to Statehood,
1748-1791,* and has written over 4,500
newspaper columns. She had poetry
published in the summer 2016 issue of the

national magazine *The Pen Woman* and in the
anthologies *Driftwood*, *Friends*, and *Perseverance*.

Barbara is a member of Space Coast Writers' Guild, Scribblers of Brevard, Florida Writers Association, the National League of American Pen Women, and the Poetry Society of Vermont. She loves writing, reading, and traveling.

HOME FOR NOW

By Beth Lambdin

What Brings You to Florida?

Since I've moved to the Sunshine State from Washington, D.C., my go-to question, whenever I meet someone new, is, "What brings you to Florida?" Recently, a lady I just met in yoga surprised me when she dismissed the woes of a brutal Calgary, Canada winter as the primary reason for her departure, and said, instead, "I love Cocoa Beach. I just do."

She is not alone. *Love* is a word people often use when they answer my informal survey. Along with that love, a certain predictability emerges from my respondents' answers. The warm weather is a big draw, of course – hordes of people delight in fleeing the frozen, snowy, blizzardy north. But just as many cite fond memories, saying they vacationed here as a child, and always wanted to live here as an adult, or that they wanted to be near family or care for aging parents.

I did meet one person, shortly after we moved to Florida, who was not over-the-top gaga about living here. When she talked about her previous home on the coast of Oregon, she lit up like a decked-out Christmas tree, all bright lights and shimmery tinsel, and it was apparent that she was not a 100% Florida gal.

Like me, her husband's job brought her here. And while she and I are certainly not hostages, we probably wouldn't have picked Florida of our own free will. She doesn't pine for her old home in any sloppy, neurotic way, but it was clear that she missed it – and her missing permitted me to miss D.C.

From Somewhere Else

"So, what brought *you* to Florida?" I sometimes get asked in return.

When I say, "My husband's job," instantly, I feel myself tumbling back into the 60s, my blunt bob morphing into a Laura Petrie flip, and my shorts and t-shirt into a plaid shirtwaist. That answer makes me sound like I orbit around my husband, Jim, (and maybe I do), and want to defend myself, although I don't have to explain that I am no man's kept woman. Jim and I married in our forties, and I supported myself just fine until then, thank you very much.

But it *was* Jim's acceptance of a job at the Kennedy Space Center that precipitated our move – although there were likely many factors that made that new job offer particularly attractive. We had grown weary of city life after nearly thirty years, the noise and the traffic (always rated as among the worst in the country), and the extra level of effort it takes to live day-to-day in a major city, and one bursting with tourists. Robust crowds dominate D.C., a good thing, overall, but still one yearns for just one spring when you can stroll around the tidal basin when the cherry trees snow pink blossoms in a brisk wind and not have to keep veering off the path to accommodate the distracted crowds. Hardly the stuff of "real" problems, yet day-after-day jockeying for space can wear you out.

And 9/11 changed D.C. for us. After the smoke

cleared from the Pentagon, which we watched burn from our front stoop in our Capitol Hill neighborhood, Jim did his best to soothe my fears with statistics about how miniscule the likelihood of catastrophic disaster really was, how the numbers were with us and supported our continued existence. But the physical changes that went up in the neighborhood – the metal bollards in front of the Capitol, the closed streets, the re-routed traffic, bag checks in the mall museums, the increased police presence, the bomb-sniffing dogs, the warnings in the subway – none of them allayed my fears. And although over time the fear grew less acute, less sharp, it was still always there, a dull ache.

Fear motivates – and it narrows the world to stark choices: fight, flight, freeze. We fled for Florida a few years later. Or did we? Maybe, just maybe, it was simply time to embark on a new adventure after three decades in familiar territory. Who in their right mind isn't seduced by beaches and palm trees?

Anticipation

While preparing to move to Florida, which went amazingly smoothly, (we sold our house in three days!), and amidst the excitement that goes with embarking on anything new, three fears troubled my sleep, waking me with a jolt – always around 3:00 a.m. They were #1: storms; #2: bugs; and last but definitely not least, #3: the scorching heat. These were, of course, in addition to my general fear of the unknown, a big bag of slime that oozed anxiety about leaving communities cultivated and tended for nearly thirty years, leaving family and aging parents, and entering a much more conservative area, where I knew not one single, solitary soul. Massaging my sore jaw after another night of clenching my teeth, I wondered: How will we ever build a solid foundation on shifting sand and porous limestone?

First Impressions

Despite the fears, we did it – we moved. On July 15, 2005, at a little after 6:00 a.m., on a D.C. morning already hot enough to prick sweat in our armpits, with our precious cargo, our geriatric cat, Hawthorne, meowing in a carrier that took up most of the folded-down storage space in the back of my fire-engine red VW Beetle, we hit the highway. Fifteen-and-a-half hours later (and one stop at a McDonald's in North Carolina, where I opened the car door and immediately stepped into dogshit), we made one right turn and one left turn and pulled into the driveway of our new home, a three-story, rented townhouse. The woman next door hailed us from her second-story porch, "I like your car!"

Basking in her positive energy, we unfolded our cramped bodies from the car, walked to the front door, turned the handle – and looked at each other in amazement. The front door was unlocked. Our mouths fell open. (Really. I saw Jim's fillings.) Clearly, we had been blown far, far away from D.C., where no one in their right mind would ever leave their front door unlocked.

We unloaded the cat, who immediately flopped down on the cool, tile floor and started to purr. His rumble comforted us. Still, the place looked and felt alien, and since the moving van was at least a day away, that night we slept on the hard floor. But, before laying our heads down, I walked to the beach, three minutes from our front door. When I saw how close we were to the beach, delight started to shove away my unease, and I pondered turning a cartwheel in the sand. I stifled that impulse, but I exhaled more fully, and my shoulders fell an inch or two from up around my ears. "Maybe this can work," I whispered into the night breeze.

Cocoa Beach (Photo by Beth Lambdin)

Just Another Day in Paradise

The first year is like a vacation that doesn't end – all lush, fecund Florida vegetation, skittering lizards, nesting sea turtles, exotic birds, rocket launches, and nearly everything (doctor, baker, grocery stores, drugstores, art museums) within a thirty-minute drive. Traffic tie-ups, a ubiquitous feature of metropolitan D.C., are a rare occurrence on the Space Coast of Central

Florida. But, so is walking, except on the beach. "The sidewalks are coming! The sidewalks are coming!" so I heard. I didn't know then that they wouldn't actually be laid for another decade, and until then coherent, physical connectors in the neighborhood would be either non-existent or pitiful, short stretches of concrete that ended abruptly in tangles of overgrown weeds and trash tossed from passing cars.

While Montana may be big sky country, Florida skies are no slouch. Here in Florida, the peachy-pinks and bruised lavenders, slate-grays and robin-egg blues are not just colors that pop on the paintings by Florine Stettheimer or Childe Hassam or Edward Hopper that hang on the walls of the National Gallery in D.C. Here in Florida, they hang overhead for daily delight. Nature is so generous to Florida.

Of course, D.C. has a lot of beauty too, with large expanses of green along the Potomac and Anacostia Rivers, and iconic memorials and monuments that remind me of our best aspirational selves. But D.C.'s lifeblood pumps on power and influence and work. Once upon a time, young and ambitious, I slipped into an obsessional work persona easily, perhaps too easily, donning navy and gray power suits and actual bow ties (for a blessedly short interval), while striving for some ephemeral *something* that would bring me ultimate satisfaction. Of course, that never happened, but it took a while to see I had way too much of my identity wrapped up in work.

But Florida, in contrast, nudges me to shift into a lower gear against a vibrant background of natural beauty that only the genuinely unconscious could miss and not appreciate.

Well, Maybe Not *Paradise*

Nowhere is perfect. While Florida has many Edenic characteristics, it falls short of Paradise. The salt air erodes our car tires and windshield wipers and the convertible top of my Mazda Miata, leaving it dull and mottled. To wash windows is futility – the salt spray smears them in hours.

And, to state the obvious, it is hot in Central Florida, a hellish feeling that you can't fully comprehend until you experience it (see anticipatory fear #3.) Organic deodorant proves useless in the beating-down-relentless sun, and I don't even have to raise my arms to smell my stinky pits. Neighbors pull me into the shade and say, "Walk before the sun rises or after it sets."

Also, as I'd feared during those sleepless nights in D.C., the bugs (see anticipatory fear #2) are things of nightmares. Hawthorne died, and we adopted a series of shorthaired cats, whose very life purpose appears to be wrapped up in bug hunting. For hours at a time, they crouch by a crack under the door to the garage waiting for a bug to amble into their territory. Occasionally, one slips by them, somehow, and when I arise in the morning, there it is, a big, old roach, lying on its back, flailing its six legs in the air. "Ew, ew," I mutter as I scramble in my pajamas to find a broom and dustpan to sweep it up and toss it out the front door before it figures out how to turn over and scuttle away.

Then there are the termites. They swarm in the

spring, which I didn't know, but learned last year, when they displaced us for four nights with our three cats while the house was tented during fumigation. Four guys in long-sleeved shirts, khaki cargo pants, and steel-toed work boots clomped around on the roof and unfurled massive gray tarps (breaking enough tiles to catalyze a reiterative nine-month cycle of leaks and black mold that soured me on living in Florida).

We moved here the year after hurricanes Charley, Frances, Ivan, and Jeanne wreaked havoc in the area (see anticipatory fear #1), and were lulled into complacency that, somehow, we were immune from hurricanes – until we weren't. Then Hurricane Matthew barreled through Florida, and we found we had underestimated just what it's like to live in a hotel room for several days and nights with three terrified cats and not know if we have a home standing and habitable when we return. We huddled in the common area of the Homewood Suites in Maitland with others displaced from their homes, my phone lighting up with texts from concerned family members and friends as the storm bore down on Cape Canaveral. But a last-minute wobble spared us, and all we had to do was go to the local Dollar Store to buy a broom and dustpan to sweep up the litter mess the cats made before we checked out.

Wherever You Go, There You Are

Coming face-to-face with my anticipated fears during the first year in this brave new world called Florida, made me vulnerable and open. I sported a favorite pink T-shirt, with a heart dead in the center, which I mended again and again as it grew increasingly holey, like some mad, obsessional tailor, refusing to give up on it and throw it away.

People are chattier in Florida. (Is that a Southern thing?) Over time, a new graciousness crept into my personal exchanges, and I factored in "chat" time at appointments. "Tell me what's going on with you," I say to my dental hygienist, and settle in to listen as she describes her twins' latest antics.

And I stuck my toe in new waters – here a writing group, there a new church, here a yoga class, there a vegetarian group – looking for like-minded, like-spirited comrades in this grand adventure.

But a lot of those new experience haven't stuck, for one reason or another. In the writing group, a guy detested pieces in the first person, and I, a personal essayist, took his detestation personally. The church's leadership cycled through a series of temporary ministers, and since I'd just gone through that in D.C., I didn't want to do it again here.

Perhaps most distressing of all was the resurgence of one of my worst character flaws, my habit of complaining. To my dismay, I discovered that Jon Kabat-Zinn is right, that *Wherever you go, there you are.* I was still me. In D.C., I complained about traffic and noise – all whirring helicopters overhead and screaming sirens on emergency vehicles careening down the street, and inconsiderate dog people. In Florida, I complain about noise, just different noise – leaf blowers, and lawn mowers, and weed whackers and buzz saws that lop off palm fronds and set my teeth on edge, and inconsiderate dog people.

Instead of the barking D.C. dogs jolting me awake in the early morning hours on the row-house porch next to our bedroom window and trampling our newly-planted pansies in the tree box out front, here in our new neighborhood, dogs bark at all hours. I slam the doors, clamp on headphones, and crank up a white-noise bamboo fountain to shut out their infernal racket. Dogs roam off-leash on the beach and snuffle turtle nests and chase shorebirds, and I want to scream what the clearly-marked signs at the entrances say, "Animals Prohibited," adding, "You inconsiderate morons! You violators of the public trust!"

There are Naughty People Everywhere

A wise woman once said to me, when I complained to her about people smoking in the bathroom at work, "There are naughty people everywhere." Indeed, there are naughty people everywhere, and unfortunately, it is taking me much longer than I thought humanly possible to stop complaining, resisting and wasting energy on things that are entirely out of my control – and matter not one whit in the whole scheme of things. I am ashamed of my smallness, my pettiness. All I have to do is watch the news for five minutes to regain perspective. I refuse to give in to my boorishness, however, and try to do my part to alleviate suffering in the world, and yet my character flaws persist. A move to Florida can only do so much. *Wherever I go, there I am.*

March for Our Lives

Which brings us to the March for Our Lives – and guns, always a fraught topic eliciting strong emotions.

On the morning of March 24, 2018, I laced up a pair of sneakers I rarely wear but chose for the additional support I hoped they would provide for the couple of miles Jim and I would walk over the Eau Gallie Causeway. After speakers fired up the crowd, we joined a couple of thousand others to raise our voices (and signs) for sensible gun safety measures. Shortly into the walk over the narrow walkway where we could barely fit side-by-side, my feet started to hurt – really hurt, so much so that it became hard to focus on anything but how much each step hurt with these damn shoes scraping my bunions.

I limped to the end of the route, nonetheless, and as we headed to our cars holding our signs (mine, "*Not Right America*," with the *N-R-A* highlighted in a black box with an image of a broken-hearted kid in the upper-right corner), a guy on the street said, "Fuck off!" when I passed him. His words hit like a fist to my gut. The march up until then had been peaceful, cars whizzing by honking support, so his hostility caught me off guard. My heart stuttered in my chest.

"Sir, can I talk to you a minute?" I asked.

He was open to that (a surprise), and we stood in front of the Eau Gallie Library, and he spat out, "You are offending five million members of the NRA with that sign."

I said, "That's not my intention. I want to express my unhappiness with the lobbying arm of the NRA and their strident opposition to sensible gun safety measures that the majority of Americans support."

"That's not what your sign says," he said.

I admitted, rather weakly that I can only fit so much on a poster.

He sensed my weakness and moved in for the kill, adamant that I was deliberately and personally offending him.

But then he asked, "What do you want?"

I told him that I wanted universal background checks, including at gun shows, to close loopholes, and he interrupted me, saying with great certainty that there are no such loopholes. I saw immediately that he and I were stuck in the weeds, with no weed whacker in sight, so I tried to shift our exchange to some little square of common ground. Surely that existed. Right?

I said, "I hear you, I do. I think the issue is much more complicated than just about guns. Like why do we grow such violent men and boys? Why do they think it's a good idea to shoot up schools and movie theatres and nightclubs and concerts and churches? Why are people feeling so alienated?"

But he wasn't ready to leave guns behind and said, "I have guns. I've always had guns. My sons have guns." He said that the government is poised to take his guns away.

I didn't know how to respond other than to say, "I don't want to take your guns away. But I can tell you that the prevalence of guns scares me. I see too that you clearly have strong feelings about this." And that seemed to release a little bit of air out of the anger balloon floating between us, that acknowledgment of his feelings. The energy shifted from spiky anger to something a tad softer, gentler, sadder.

As he talked, I kept trying to place his accent. "Where are you from?" I asked.

"Zambia," he said, adding, "Once you lose rights, you never get them back."

Now, *that* was interesting. We parted company after a few more minutes, amicably, no small thing given where we started. But I was rattled walking away. I wondered: was my position unfair, too reductive? Maybe. But I wondered too about his perspective as an outsider. That part I can relate to – being the outsider. Florida often feels like a foreign country to me, given its scorching climate, fierce storms, fractious politics, strident gun advocacy, and legacy of oppression, including the disenfranchisement of over a million felons who have served their time.

And there was a certain renegade quality to the exchange that felt so Florida to me, after steeping myself in the local culture for thirteen years. There is a definite, "Fuck You!" freedom of expression here, and something else too: a sense of entitlement that says, *I am going to do what I want, when I want, and you can't do anything about it*, which feels menacing – and kind of exhilarating. Just what that guy from Zambia embodied.

The Shape of Place

At home, I googled Zambia and read about its history as Northern Rhodesia, its legacy of colonial racism, its natural beauty including spectacular Victoria

Falls on the border with Zimbabwe, and I wondered how much a place shapes the way we are. How is Florida shaping me? Is living here making me more courageous, more willing to step out of my comfort zone and engage with a gun-loving guy from a country on the other side of the world? Is residing among surfers whose lifestyle (baffling to me) allows them to leave work in the middle of the day to hop on surfboards and ride the waves making me more flexible?

I hope so.

Certainly, living in Florida invites me to look at things differently, providing lots of opportunities to not condemn others, but to try to understand them and reach some common ground. For instance, while I still don't like the canines on the beach, I don't hurl invective at the owners, I just pass on by, and most days don't even think particularly dark thoughts about them. And there are actually times when I kind of get a kick out of watching the doggy energy on full display – the pup biting at the leash, the obvious affection between man and beast. I can relate. Who doesn't feel restricted at times? Who doesn't long for doggie devotion? Maybe the dogs have something to teach me – if I can just get past that they are where I don't think they ought to be.

Home for Now

Part of me did not know how urban I was until I left D.C. Now, when I return, I play tourist at the Supreme Court, the Library of Congress and the Capitol. I suspect that, similarly, I don't fully appreciate Florida while I am in the midst of it.

For now, the beach is my D.C., a place of refuge, a democratic place where all are welcome, regardless of color, creed, religion, sexual orientation, political beliefs, or views on guns. At the beach, there is diversity, people of many hues, from tawny brown to ebony black, to sun-burned red and ghostly white. Women covered head-to-toe recline next to uncovered women in skimpy, thong bikinis. Guys with enormous bellies swig Buds next to guys with hard abs rippling under suntan oil. The scent of coconut and Coppertone hangs in the air. And kids are kids, the great equalizer. They all squeal that same universal piercing shriek and turn cartwheels in the sand and wriggle with delight. A little girl in a hot pink swimsuit twirls in a frenzy of excitement she cannot contain. She stops and staggers like she is besotted.

And, yes, I still get pissed when visitors leave trash behind and bring their dogs to the beach and let them poop and don't clean up after them and let them chase after wildlife and snuffle in sea turtle nests and no one does anything about it. But that's life here. I can delight in the delights – the skittering crabs, the darting birds, the lumbering sea turtles, the jaw-dropping sunsets, the purity of the air after a terrific storm, the frisson of satisfaction I get spearing plastic out of the ocean with my rusty picker – and shrug off the unimportant. Or like that same wise woman once said to me, I can let the small stuff rob my joy and curdle into resentments.

My choice. Because, ultimately, D.C., Florida, it doesn't matter. No matter where I am, I am, and there will likely always be an underlying tension between all that is good and all that can be good. My Florida is just one hot, sub-tropical version of a not-yet-fully-realized ideal. Harmony awaits in the wings – like a benevolent spirit until I get there.

Some days, when I walk on the beach, the winds are so fierce, so brutally punishing that my first impulse is to give up, trudge home and sulk. Instead, I shut my mouth to stop eating the wind-blown sand and persevere. I am always glad that I do. The winds help stop the incessant mind chatter and force me to be here, fully here, NOW.

I've been so resistant, so reluctant to call Florida "home." But calling it anything *but* home after thirteen years seems plain silly.

"So, what brings you to Florida?" someone will inevitably ask me in the not-too-distant future. My first impulse will be to tell them too much, more than they want to hear. Rather than watch their eyes glaze over, perhaps a better response will be to say, "Come walk on the beach with me, and you will see for yourself why I came – and why I stay."

# # #

Beth Lambdin is a non-fiction writer, essayist, memoirist, and award-winning film critic. She has reviewed films for *The Voice of the Hill*, *The Senior Beacon* and the *Washington Window*. She has  been published in *The Washington Post*, *Orlando Sentinel, The Leader Herald, Natural Awakenings*, and several SCWG anthologies. She is currently working on a collection of personal essays. Beth lives in Cocoa Beach, FL, with her husband, Jim, and their three cats. Visit her online at www.melambdin.com.

FOR MY AIS ONLY

By Richard Marschall

Breaking News! First Warning Alert! The announcement broke over the airwaves, followed immediately by the appearance of Channel 13's Chief Meteorologist Ted Wronka, with a grim look on his face.

"Good afternoon! The National Weather Bureau has just issued an extreme weather alert for most of Central Florida and Brevard County for this evening and into the overnight. For the next 24 hours Central Florida and the Space Coast, all the way down to Vero, will be under a heightened state of emergency with the potential for severe weather. Heavy rains, dangerous winds, hail and tornadic activity and swells four to six feet above normal cannot be ruled out for most of the night. Storm Tractor 13 will track this storm closely as it makes its way across the state. Please stand by for ..."

The old set crackled and blinked twice before shutting down. *How many times had I told the old man to fork out the money for a new flat screen TV? Do you think he would listen? Just like everything else in his life, it was a big joke.*

I thought that was going to be it – no TV or news for the rest of the evening. But a minute later the archaic Magnavox crackled back to life and my old sweetheart, Meghan McGloin, popped up on the screen. Five-foot-seven, with long, silky, auburn hair, blue eyes, and pouty lips, she had the fine-honed physique of a gymnast and the demeanor of a delicate porcelain doll. She reminded me of Angelica Jolie in her role in the Final Apocalypse movie.

Meghan and I had been sweethearts through high school until she met Steve, the tall blond-haired captain of the football team and president of the debate club. As if that wasn't enough, he was also the son of one of the wealthiest car dealers in Melbourne.

There was no question I would have married Meghan. My Dad told me I'd be the luckiest guy on Earth if Meghan stayed with me. I'll never know because she didn't stay around that long. And though Mom didn't do it intentionally, her aloofness and arrogance created barriers between Meghan and me. No one was *ever* right for her one and only son.

I was crushed when Meghan told me she wouldn't be seeing me more anymore. I told no one of my hurt. For many months, my grief hung in the air like a bad mold, simmering and growing worst; and then it was gone. I never confided to my new girlfriend the deep secret I harbored. I hoped that somehow, someday, someway, the fire might be rekindled. For years, I made believe it didn't matter.

***

As the young, female meteorologist sashayed over to the large studio weather map, all eyes were focused on the highlighted bright red and yellow areas of the storm front to the west of us. Pointing to the dense mass that was headed in our direction, Meghan continued soberly: "We must caution. This is a very unusual storm with the potential to cause significant damage. Oceanic pressure has already dropped below 879 mlb., only 9 points higher than the lowest reading ever recorded. I cannot overemphasize the magnitude of this storm. Coupled with an extremely volatile high-pressure system to the west, we have the ingredients for the perfect storm. Brevard County hasn't seen anything like this for well over a hundred years."

Looking directly into the camera, McGloin went on: "For the next 24 hours Central Florida will be under a heightened State of Emergency, with a 100% probability of strong winds, heavy rains, thunderstorms, occasional large hail, swells 4 – 6 feet over normal and severe tornadic activity. Low-lying areas will suffer flooding, and there will be significant beach erosion. Governor Rick Scott has issued warnings for motorists to stay off the roads and placed the National Guard on Standby should they be needed. The Governor has also issued a 10:00 p.m. curfew for residents living beachside."

Chances were the newscasters were overstating the outcome for their ratings. Losers! Half the time they didn't get the weather right and the other half, they were downright wrong. The weather down here seldom lived up to the hype. Besides, I didn't give a sand fleas' butt what they said! If conditions provided me the opportunity to locate the missing Indian mounds I'd been looking for, I would take the risk! If my hunches were right, and my research accurate, this might be my big night! To heck with the weather!

Call me crazy, or maybe obsessed, but this was something I *had* to do. The idea of finding something new was in my blood. The O'Hearns were an arrogant bunch. We were the VIP's of the New World – the "chosen" ones. My forefathers had come to America with Columbus. They would *not* have shirked from this task. Da Gama, Lewis and Clark, Amundsen - where would they have been if they gave up before they began. My great-great-great... grandfather's portrait had adorned our living room wall for as long as I could remember. Isaac O'Hearn *would* have pushed on. A deckhand, but by all rights, a man of honor. He would have been right there with me if he were still alive.

Father never spoke to me of the family, our lineage or "privilege." It was my mother who instilled in me a fierce pride for my ancestors - her many, many, "great, greats". She taught me to look down on others who didn't share our heritage. I was torn between my father's ambivalence and my mother's profound loyalty to a group of people I didn't even know. And, although I didn't understand the full implications and complexities of the theory, I felt as if I was caught at some level of Einstein's "EPR Paradox" – always a part of, yet never quite the solution to the conundrum. I craved acknowledgment from my father but needed approval from mom. He did not notice the times I turned away or sobbed quietly into little cupped hands. I grew to hate the false pretenses and innuendos of the Rosales' family. There were many times I did not talk to either parent for weeks.

***

The bitterness and anger manifested itself in times of self-pity and suffocation. But bitterness turned to

160

rage and suffocation to defiance. I no longer needed their love or approval. When I didn't get my way I would scream, or jump up and down, throw things, or worse. I too, like my mother, became arrogant; but in so doing, I lost something – my humanity. I no longer cared what others thought or what I had to do to get my way. I held my head high and forged on regardless of cost.

***

I could hardly wait to get started. My eyes must have been as big as saucers. My heart was beating like a drum in anticipation of possibly finding a mitten, one of the ancient Indian trash mounds. That's *all* I wanted. My discovery didn't have to be monumental. The relics and artifacts would prove once and for all my hypothesis on the existence of an Ais settlement in this part of the peninsula. It would be my crowning achievement. I would have the material for my book. I would not have to teach lowly undergraduate courses to unthankful freshmen and sophomores at the State college anymore.

Visiting Associate Professor at Eastern Florida University, teaching Early Florida History and Archaeology of Eastern Florida, Jason Rosales stood 6' 1" in height, with medium brown hair and a light bounce in his step. His catching personality and almost charismatic presentations had made him an instant star on campus, and his courses were always booked. "Professor Rosales' courses are so interesting. It's like being inside the heads of the people he's talking about." His students said this on more than one occasion.

The elusive history of the vanished Ais had interested Jason for many years. He had stumbled upon the ancient tribe back in high school when one of his instructors had made a brief mention of them in class. Four years ago, he had been to the Pentoaya Town site in Melbourne which had been conclusively designated as the "Winter-Time" Ais settlement in this part of Florida. The unveiling of its $2,500 metal marker was a momentous turning point in his life. Earlier research had led him to believe that somewhere further south another such town existed. The Pentoaya Marker substantiated his findings. Perhaps tonight would be *his* night of discovery. In his heart, the reality of what he was doing told a different story. *"These darn Indians have been the bane of my life. They get more credit for their imagined existence than I get for all my degrees."*

***

Storm warnings had been issued ahead for the big storm. I was certain no one other than myself be on the beach tonight. The beach would be deserted, and I would be alone. There would be no one to help me if I ran into problems. *Columbus was on his own – there was no one else would or could make the momentous decisions that were to shape America's destiny. Was I any different than Columbus?*

***

My father sat languidly in his torn, faded, olive-green Lazy-Boy. This was his favorite chair and the throne no one dared touch. We lived under the same roof and in the same small two thousand square foot rancher, but that was about all. We spoke on occasion, but normally he went his way and I went mine. We'd lived together since 2013 when my mom died of a cerebral clot that never found its way out of her skull. Ocean Avenue, Melbourne Beach Florida, wasn't a bad place to live.

Dad had taken mom's death hard. His emaciated hands told the whole story. He just *existed*. No more, no less. "Pop," I announced at the last minute, "I'm going to the beach tonight." His expression said it all. He knew! *Knew* that it was my project again. "Maybe the storm will wash something up," I continued, averting my eyes from his glare.

"I guess it wouldn't do no good to tell you not to go," he said in his feeble voice. "I can't remember the last time you listened to anything I had to say anyway." I hesitated for an instant, just enough time for him to get in his last barb. "There's a bad storm coming our way. Can't you just forget about your *stupid* research for a while?"

I was going to turn and say something, but I thought the better of it. What good would it do? I walked quickly out the blue, splintered, wood-paneled door and headed toward the beach. It was only a couple blocks, and the exercise would do me good.

The Atlantic glistened under what was left of the new Florida moon – a moon that would soon be blanketed by dark clouds and obscene rain. It was like a Highwayman painting, exquisite, yet ominous in its detail. Harold Newton had done himself proud. It would not last long. Soon the sky would turn pitch-black dark, with ominous blue-purple-black clouds obscuring the view altogether.

The crash of the waves and the approaching thunder

put my nerves on edge and my senses on high alert. This was crazy! I shouldn't be out here! What the devil was I thinking? If lightning struck, no one would find me until morning.

I visualized my father in his worn, discolored Lazy-Boy, the morning paper spread out on the divan and his library books on the floor. He'd be asleep by 9:00 p.m. What if *he* had a problem? What if he died? Did I *care*?

I thought this might be a good time to text Lauren:

Me: beach 2nite. Heading s. Winds picking up. rains 2 b heavy. good feeling about 2nite. Dangerous conditions. Old man's at home in his chair. Text me

Lauren: My mother warned me about boys like u. lol. why can't u do your research in the day like everyone else when sun's out and sky's clear? r u going to c me firday?

Me: Spelling! Bad! Lol! Can't! Lot 2 do! Wish me well! micco promising. Lots Work. Got 2 go. Talk 2 u latr! L.U. J

I wasn't sure if I even cared for this girl. It was more like she was just someone there to fill in the void.

***

I had come to the beach as I always did – right before the storm and the tide. The shore yielded its most bounteous riches with the incoming tides.

I walked quickly to cover as much territory as I could before the storm - further than usual this time – almost down to Micco. A few more yards I would have been *in* Micco. My dream for more years than I can remember has been to uncover one of the ancient middens or garbage dumps of the Ais. I would give anything to be able to sort through their pottery, shards, and artifacts. *Dumb Indians get all the credit!*

Mom's last words were to stand proud, take charge, and stand behind my convictions. Dad just kind of stood back and let life come as it would. I was the composite and product of this mixed, dyslexic marriage.

***

The thunder crashed, and a bolt of lightning lit up the northern sky. The storm was right on course. I would have to go right through it to get home. I shivered to think of walking the unlit, narrow beach back to Ocean Ave. The tide was coming in fast, and a large chunk of the beach was already inundated in the waves. The rains started quickly, making visibility virtually impossible. I didn't care! It was just me, the sands and the waves! If only they would wash up an ancient mound, all this would be worth my hardship and risk. *No one would care if I was lost or harmed.* I felt my temples pounding - a migraine had started. What is wrong with me? I've got a great job, a roof over my head, a wonderful, caring girlfriend and been to all the places I've ever dreamed. Yet I looked down on the very people who meant anything to me. It was no different than using the Mullet for the Snook. Once it had served its purpose, it no longer had any value.

My flashlight barely lit up a dozen feet in front of me. The froth was stinging my eyes, and the dropping temperatures shot through me like a hurricane wind.

My tee was soaked, and hardly enough protection as the temperatures plummeted. The thermometer must have dropped twenty degrees in the last hour. I wasn't prepared for the storm this was sizing up to be.

I looked at the sea, or what I thought was the sea. There was no line where the depths met the land. I was becoming disoriented. The sky had become black and the waters opaque. I ran, scared and trembling, unsure of my footing, reckless in my desperation. I tripped on a root in the sand and struck my head on an outcropping of beach rock. I must have fallen and lain in the rain for a dozen minutes or more before I awoke and continued in the storm.

I hadn't gone far when my vista changed. Everything was now circumscribed by groups of scantily clad people to my front, my rear and my sides. They were dark-skinned with long black hair and the most exquisite features; except for one, who stood out from the rest, obviously much older and wizened by time. A godlike figure, standing tall and erect, sporting beautiful, long white hair that hung down over his powerful shoulders; his omniscience that of a Zeus.

Each Indian wore braided necklaces of seashells, and loincloths for cover. They were a hardy, wiry people. The woman appeared better fed than the warriors. The few maidens I saw also had long, black hair, and feigned an innocence worthy of a Cleopatra. Most of the men carried wooden bows and knives carved out of a shell.

It was apparent that they had just returned from an expedition for seafood and berries. They carried with them poles of fish and bowls of blueberries and other fruits I did not recognize. They were happy, and though circumspect at my intrusion, seemed eager to get on with their feast.

Strangely, the rains had stopped, and the night was still, in the company of these beautiful Indians.

They came upon me as a group. Seeing my fear, the blueness of my skin and the goosebumps I tried to hide, they covered me in a warm animal skin, possibly deer. The fur was soft, though the hide not so pliant. A man whom I deemed to be the chief gave signals to two older women to come to comfort me and to make me feel at ease.

They offered me berries and shellfish and plants I didn't know. A maiden held onto each arm and led me into one of the thatched huts lined up on the beach. I watched as they set their wares on tables also constructed of thatch and as they placed their gourdes and bowls of shell and bones on the table before me. I ate until I was full and then laid down on a mat of palm reeds, before falling to sleep. It was all here, the utensils, the relics of the past, the discarded shells and musical instruments, and the fabulous dishes and bowls of these magnificent, primitive peoples of the distant past.

***

They were unlike any people I'd ever seen before - and I had traveled to the far ends of the world: Fiji, Borneo, Tierra del Fuego, the Galapagos... There was something different about these people, a presence, an aura, something that set them apart. I couldn't quite place my thoughts around it yet. My head still throbbed, and I was groggy to boot. My migraine had intensified. Seeing my pain, they offered me herbs which I took, gulping them down with a strange wine I couldn't identify. They made me feel at home, at ease, unburdened of my anxieties. I wished to stay with them, to remain in this fantasy.

A computer screen, much like my own HP crackled, and strange images appeared. *I had left my computer at home. Where did they get this computer? This wasn't happening!* Yet it was, and the Chief was typing some strange language into the computer, waiting for it to respond. A bluish glow and indefinable haze made it difficult to focus. *What in the world was going on?*

Diagrams and hieroglyphics appeared on the screen. It was as nothing I had ever seen. Sounds I didn't recognize emanated from the speaker. I touched the table to make sure it was real. It swayed under my touch. I felt lightheaded, my thoughts disorganized. One of the Indian maidens spoke to me in accented English. She was beautiful; exotic and esoteric, unlike anyone I'd ever met before. Her words calmed me, and her touch was gentle and reassuring. I sat down, unsure of what might happen next. *I* certainly wasn't guiding the situation. The fact of the matter was, the fluidity of the situation was out of my hands.

Shortly, the person whom I believed to be the Chief abruptly stopped what he was doing on the computer and walked over to me. This tall, gaunt, commanding figure looked at me sternly before he spoke. "Jason Rosales, we have known about you and your work for a long time. You must understand that we mean you no harm."

I was beginning to get a little scared; the hairs on the backs of my hands and arms stood on end. His voice sent chills down my spine, and though I had no visible cause for alarm, his words belied an ulterior motive for his conversation. "Tell me what it is you want from me," I said.

He repeated. "We mean you no harm, but you *must* cease your quest."

"What are you talking about?" I queried, unsure of where this was going. "I've spent my entire life searching for you people and I'm not giving up now!" I said, exhaling loudly for all to hear. I looked directly at the older man. I could almost visualize the vessels in my face popping to the surface, my eyes wide in disbelief. Shaking my fist at the Chief, I felt my life unraveling before me.

With a wave of his hand, he stopped me and repeated: "The Ais, as you call us, are a peaceful people. We mean no one any harm. We only left because you Earthlings were getting too close. Others may not understand it was not out of fear. We *have* the means to annihilate any foe."

Panic was beginning to register as beads of sweat formed on my brow; my frame shook uncontrollably. "Are you *not* from here?" I already knew the answer before I asked.

"It is a long story Earthling, and one that time does not allow us to share now. We are from a far-away place and like many people in Florida's past, only pilgrims. We came to your peninsula seeking the promise of a better land - sun, sustenance, and peace. For many years, before other hostile tribes came, we lived in harmony with the land and the sea. For hundreds of years, we thought we could co-exist...." He stopped.

I couldn't help myself. "But... what happened?"

"These early Americans weren't content with *some* of the great lands of the Peninsula. They wanted it *all*. They treated the lands and the waters as if they belonged to them. There were fights and scuffles. Our peoples were driven from their farms, hunting grounds, and fishing spots. Many were killed and suffered horrible atrocities at the hands of the strangers. And then came the peoples in the big, wooden boats."

"You mean the Europeans? You just gave it all up?" I asked incredulously.

"We attempted to live in harmony with the lands and the new settlers, but it wasn't meant to be. Our mandate had been to live in peace. Only through love, compassion and grace was our small contingent allowed to stay in this new Eden. Without the ability to defend ourselves and our lands, our tribes grew smaller and smaller. We soon found we no longer had the population to sustain ourselves and sent a message across the stars for our leaders to come to take us home. We chose hunger, tainted air, and a stagnant economy rather than the ravages of war and decimation. So, there you have it. Not weakness, but fortitude, and our resolve to fulfill the promise to our leaders who had accorded us this opportunity for a new beginning. It had been decreed, as part of our covenant, that the Ais could never use their advanced technology to win the day. You must *never* relate any of what I tell you to another soul."

"You can still live here. I'll get an exception for you. This can become "tribal lands." I will publish a book about you, and everyone will know of your plight, and I will become famous," I cried out, regretting what I said before the last word came out of my mouth.

The maidens cried, and the warriors shook their heads. I didn't care! I was adamant I was going to present my findings in the national journals and news magazines. No one was going to stop me from my quest. *No one cared about these few Indians and their problems. This was the story of a lifetime! And I was going to claim it! No one was going to deprive me of what I had honestly earned.*

The maiden, whom I learned was called "Dawn," pulled me to the side and kissed me on the lips. I could smell her heavy bouquet and feel her leathered skin. She was gentle and pliable in my arms. I let myself slip into the ambiance of the moment. Only for a second, I experienced a feeling like never-before – I was enraptured in the presence of this simple woodland creature, in love with a ghost, an idea, a perfection. I was frozen in a place not of my choosing – the subtleties of an electric I never knew.

The Chief wasn't as gentle, though not by any means rough. He led me to the computer and a video playing on the screen. In an instant, I was enveloped in what appeared to be an outdoor IMAX. It was all he had. It was a chronicle of the Ais. It depicted their modest beginnings, their development and at the finale, their horrible, tragic end. I was speechless as I watched their story unfold and dumbfounded as I watched their final demise. Something happened to me in that brief span of time that I will never be able to explain - freedom like I'd only experienced once before when I presented an essay that had taken me many weeks to write, to my sixth-grade class on Dr. Martin Luther King's kindness and compassion. My outlook did a 180 degree about-face, and my philosophy changed that night after viewing the incredible journey of these magnificent people. I understood their plight, their journey, and pain. I was *part* of their exodus, their presence and part of their tribe. I no longer wished to reveal to the world the secrets of these incredible people, for I understood it would hurt them far more than it would provide material benefits to me.

It was then I realized that the images I was watching and the voices I heard were only projected 4-D holographic video and audio. None of this was real. The fact was, no one was here anymore. Yet it *was* real, projected across light years of the universe.

The old chief attempted a smile. It may as well have been a sneer. Waiting a long moment, he gave his final parting statement: "Jason Rosales, what you are seeing and hearing is a reality far beyond your Earthly senses. Our scientists have developed the means to project 4-D images and sounds across the universe in the time it takes to blink an eye. Images that you see are essentially real and are manipulated much as you play your silly game videos on Earth."

"But enough! You must trust the veracity of my words when I tell you that it is only because of your empathy and understanding the Mother Ship is returning to Earth a final time. Our advanced technology enables us to look into the future. We knew of your work and imminent discovery many years ago. Five years ago we began the process of formulating plans to contact you to try to dissuade you from announcing the results of your research. We knew changing your mind would be a monumental task. One as hardheaded and determined as yourself might never change, but it was worth a try. We waited for a moment when you could see us as we were. The massive storm provided us the opportunity, and your fall, the occasion to execute our plan. We knew if we could demonstrate our love and goodwill you might reciprocate. It was our only chance."

"How'd I do?" I asked laughingly.

"We thought we had learned everything of the human psyche until we met you. You proved us wrong and changed our whole perspective. Our leaders made the unheard-of decision to allow us to return to Earth one final time to request your presence on our home planet. Had it not been for you, Jason Rosales, we would have never returned. Our time from home to Earth and time on Earth and back has been a long, incredible journey spanning many of your Earth years. Though I know it is hard to understand, we are having this conversation with you two and a half years ago. Tomorrow we will embark on our mission to your planet for the final time. Space is a vast area, and there is an incredible distance we must travel to reach Earth. Once we enter deep space, our bodies will be immersed in hypobaric chambers, which will enable us to make the two and a half year journey from home to your Earth. Cryo-technology has enabled this miracle. Once we arrive at the outer limits of your solar system, we will make contact. We won't have long to remain this time."

"Do not worry Jason. You will have many, many more years. Like us, you will live for hundreds of years in perfect health. Our planet, our people, live in harmony with the lands and each other and though we may not have material riches, we are wealthy in the bounteous treasures of the mind and the spirit. Should you decide to return with us, you will have only two days to prepare after we enter Earth's atmosphere. Be well. The adventure awaits." That was the last I heard of the Ais for nine hundred and one days until they entered our solar system.

***

The Ais had dropped a no-brainer in my lap! These people had given me an opportunity I didn't deserve, a chance at a new life. I felt like weights had been removed from my ankles, shackles cast from a lifetime of contentious opposites. It was as if heavy wool blankets were removed from my body in the dead of summer; like chugging down some smooth Columbian coffee during the coldest day of winter. A new freedom lifted me, like downy feathers in a fresh zephyr of ocean air. Two and a half years would be a small price to pay to share in the boundless riches of the universe.

# # #

Richard Marschall has been writing in one form or another his entire life, whether it be poetry, epic poetry, short stories, novels, or non-fiction. He  graduated from Towson University and did his graduate work at Western Illinois University. He is a member of Scribblers of Brevard, Space Coast Writers' Guild, the Florida Writers Association, and Poetry Soup, an online poetry forum. He has had a number poems published in various anthologies. His book, *First Call – Poetry for the Ages*, was published in 2018.

RIDERS ON THE STORM

By Heddy McCoy

John emerged from below-deck in time to see his father trail the back of his hand down the small of the mermaid statue's back, then bend to give her a hard shake at the bottom of her upturned fin to make sure she was securely lashed at the bow. His father whispered behind the mermaid's ear, "Good morning, Marjie, I hope you're ready for our trip."

It was quiet in the marina except for the occasional slap of water along the side of the nearby boats. *The Caroline* swayed as John dropped his overnight bag across the side onto the dock, ready to throw in the car for the drive north. He stepped back and down into the cockpit just as Buzz came forward with two plastic cups with shots of bourbon. It was a ritual that they had shared before every trip since John had turned 15. As they had already gone through the motions of gassing up the boat, pumping out the head, and had filled up with ice yesterday evening, Buzz was ready to set sail this morning, and all that was left was to say goodbye.

"You'll call when you're close to Melbourne?"

Nodding slightly, Buzz raised his cup, "To Marjie."

"To Mom," John replied.

They pulled the bumpers on board, and John stepped onto the dock.

"Dad, one more time - wait out the hurricane season to take her out?" Already knowing the answer, he started to untie the lines to the dock and push on the boat.

"I'm finally ready to let her go," he motioned his bourbon cup to the statue, as he pulled the lines aboard.

"I swear you have a death wish," John muttered under his breath.

"Give those grandsons of mine big hugs from their old Grandpa," he winked as he turned the key and the motor sputtered to life.

"And give your sister a call for me, would you? Tell her I'll call when I get there?"

John waved him off and stayed a little longer than he needed to as he watched his father motor out from the basin and finally saw the sails blossom on the horizon.

***

Buzz woke up one day and got it in his craw; he could think of nothing else. The thought of dying and rejoining Marjie in the great beyond was replaced by his newfound purpose to take the statue to sea. He didn't care about any storms; he didn't care that the boat was old and he was older still. He didn't care that *Caroline's* radio didn't work. He had a job to do for her.

Her ashes had been split into three, a divine number, Marjie had said. One third was in the plot of land beneath a shared headstone in the cemetery where his children knew to put his ashes with her. One third was buried below a newer Live Oak in the backyard, joining the ashes of her beloved Golden Retriever, Sammy. She said he could talk to her there anytime he wanted, and besides, those trees lasted forever, and she had imagined children a hundred years from now playing on her branches. Sammy did love kids. They could watch them play together. The final third was sent and mixed into a concrete and pumice mixture and formed into many statues by a company specializing in these kinds of things. There were the two small ones that resembled coral for mantles - the kids each had one. The bigger one of the three statues was in the form of a mermaid statue, now gracing the front of his boat, that he would drop to the ocean floor so she could watch fish swim around for her for years to come.

So, here he was. The heavy base of the statue was cut with a V in the back, so the statue rested evenly balanced above the prow. At least he wouldn't have to hoist her over the lines since he was making this sail alone. He could just unlash her, give her a push, and she'd be overboard. On their test sails, just as he did now, Buzz imagined himself a Viking with the lucky mermaid figurehead watching the journey.

He hoped to stay out on the ocean as much as possible, though he would sail into the Intercoastal Waterway and anchor overnight at some of the clubs where his club in the Keys shared reciprocity. The plan was to make his way north to the Sebastian Inlet where he'd enter the Indian River toward Melbourne. The Melbourne club also had reciprocity and his son was a member there too. If he got there in time, *The Caroline* already had a buyer in snowbirds wintering there. There was a smaller boat that he already had his eye on, with better gadgets that would make it easier for him to manage.

Now he was out, blue sky and towering clouds stretched in front of him as far as he could see and though there were some winds, the sails were manageable. He and Marjie had taken this sail together not ten years ago, and he had done it a few times on his own since. It wouldn't be a problem. In all honesty, *The Caroline* wasn't too hard to manage on his own, but he was getting older and was exhausted when he put in at Fort Lauderdale for some shut-eye. If he hadn't known before, he should have known there. Instead, he woke late and anxious to be on his way, he hurried out, barely speaking to anyone as he left. He missed the club chatter about the storm headed their way.

***

He couldn't stop laughing. He couldn't stop crying. At least Marjie's statue made it to the bottom of the ocean. Her statue, his phone, his supplies, his warm clothes, and unfortunately his boat were all at the bottom of the ocean. He had snagged a life vest and had been floating for less than an hour now, but losing feeling in his legs was probably a bad sign. He had swallowed a lot of salt water, inhaling it from waves that were getting angrier and angrier.

His head nodded down to rest on his orange vest toward sleep when he felt something bumping him from below. Vaguely he wondered if sharks would venture to the surface for food in this kind of storm, but no, there were two dolphins next to him. Incredulous, but too tired to be anything but thankful, they nudged him until he took hold of one of their dorsal fins. He took turns holding on to each of them as they pulled him forward. He only hoped it was closer to shore.

He realized there was a boat tossing in the waves ahead of him, and he made out on the stern that it was *The Cuki* from Rochester, New York. More important, it hadn't sunk yet. It was a little bigger than *The Caroline*. Their sails weren't even up. He started yelling at the people on board who were probably trying their best not to get tossed into the ocean. They didn't hear him over the storm. The boat was farther away than it looked and it took what seemed a lifetime to get there as he and the dolphins were battered by the waves. When they finally got close, he reached out and was just barely able to grasp hold of the bottom rung of the ladder to pull himself up. His rescue was almost thwarted again when midway through his climb, the ass of the boat bucked high in the air. It took everything he had to hold on as it slammed back down into the ocean. The dolphins were gone.

Pulling himself into the cockpit, he realized the unhelpful Captain and his guests were really mannequins lashed to the boat. Two men (one with a missing head) and three women were sitting together and posed like they were getting ready to take a selfie. Freaky.

Below deck, there were some dry clothes and rain gear and even blankets on the bed in the berth which he donned to keep warm until the feeling started to come back to his legs and hands. The radio was dead. Boat essentials and non-essentials were tossing back and forth on the floor, rolling and sliding hard into his feet and shins, including a CD that he bent over and scooped up – a *Best of the Doors* compilation. He fired on the stereo which did work and cranked the volume as loud as he could. Jim Morrison's crooned, and suddenly he felt like he wasn't alone.

After a couple of swigs from the bottle of rum that he found in a still-lashed cupboard, he swished the dark silk around in his mouth and spat in the galley sink before stowing it. Some of the lines that were sliding back and forth on the floor would do to lash himself to the side of the boat. He took a seat next to the mannequins. They had made it mostly unscathed on this side of the boat, so maybe it would be good luck. At least he'd have good tunes and quiet company.

It was a good thing he had the rain gear, he decided. He was almost never seasick, but with his earlier swallowing of seawater and the current tossing of the boat, his upchuck factor was at a level of 12 out of 10. With the ocean spray doing clean-up, he was happy the sick rolled off the yellow rubber after it hit him across his belly. At some point, the waves hit hard enough that another one of the mannequins lost her head. He floated in and out of consciousness, but the boat was holding.

Whining woke him. A wet Golden Retriever was now on the boat and nudging his knee. "Wakey wakey, Sleepyhead."

Some part of him knew it couldn't be real. "Marjie? What the hell? Am I dead?"

She was wearing that blue sundress that he loved and was sitting across from him on the empty bench

182

getting drenched. She raised her eyebrows, telling him to get a grip and turned to examine his new friends sitting next to him. "Well, this is one way to spend a Tuesday, Babe."

Sammy jumped up onto his bench to get to his lap, spreading across the mannequins and knocking the headless guy's arm off with his tail wagging. "Seriously - not dead?" She shook her head.

"Marj, I'm so sorry. I lost *The Caroline.*"

"It's just a boat. I'm angrier about you coming out like this. You're a seasoned sailor, for God's sake, Buzz, and it is the middle of hurricane season. And don't you dare blame me or my mermaid - it isn't my fault you acted like you had a death wish."

Even with the wind whipping around her, the light of the hurricane eye haloed behind her. All he could do was choke out, "I miss you so much."

Petting Sammy and taking her in, his tears joined the driving rain, and he somehow realized he was surprised he had any tears left to cry. She walked to him unfazed by his grief or the storm and sat on his lap, wrapping her arms around his neck.

Sun and blue sky replaced the dark gray clouds. While the waves were still choppy, the lack of a relentless downpour in his face was calming. His dead wife in his arms was calming. She untied his hood and pushed it down from his forehead, running fingers through his hair and leaned in to kiss him.

Scrambling to untie the lines while still lip-locked,

he stood them up, and she stepped back.

She waved her finger at him and only telling him, "No."

"It isn't time yet. Take care of the kids. Call Becca more, please. You can't just talk to John - she needs you."

"I will, I promise."

"Buzz, live your life. Talk to people. Dance. You're a great dancer."

She talked as she stripped to her slip, then smiled, took a step up, mouthed "I love you" and dove off the side of *The Cuki.* She was splashing around with what he could have sworn were the two dolphins that had saved him earlier.

Before he could join her, she yelled at him, "It is coming again, lash yourself up for God's sake, man!" A mermaid dive hid her below the dark water.

"Goddamnit, Marjie! Come back!"

A huge wave barreled toward the boat as they approached the edge of the eye, and he ran back to the seat, tying the knots as tight as he could. He'd go down with the ship if it came to that, but he wouldn't get tossed off of it. He held on tight to Sammy as the giant wave slammed into them.

***

He was face-down, and a dog's wet nose and sandpaper tongue licked him into consciousness. He coughed and took in a mouthful of sand.

"Baxter!" he heard someone call. He was on land. He rolled over and reached down to feel his limbs. He seemed to be fully intact even though he felt like someone had beaten him from head to toe with a baseball bat. He opened his eyes and slowly sat up.

"Hey Dude, are you okay?" a homeless-looking man with a long beard and board shorts asked him as he pulled the dog away and as Buzz pulled seaweed off of his legs.

"I guess I'm not dead. At least, I don't think I'm dead. You're not Jesus are you?" Buzz asked.

"Well some people do call me Beach Jesus, but no, I'm not Jesus."

"Buzz," he said, extending his hand.

"Like the astronaut?" Buzz nodded. He peeled off his raincoat and rested his elbows on his knees and looked around. "Where am I?"

"On the barrier island in Melbourne Beach. That's in Florida. There's a golf course called Spessard Holland just behind us with a pretty nice public restroom." Beach Jesus told him.

"Hey, pretty nice boat you have there."

"That? That's not mine," he said, looking over to see *The Cuki* resting on the beach as if it had been picked up by the hand of God and intentionally placed there. "Um, do you have a cell phone?"

"Sure do, you have someone you can call?" he said, handing over his cell.

"Thanks, yes – it's a local call."

He was lucky he remembered the number. He called John to come to get him at the beach by the place they had golfed last time he was in town. John was under strict instructions to also bring food, dry clothes, and cash for Beach Jesus. Buzz had to promise his son that he would tell him the whole story and that was physically okay only about eighty times before John would let him hang up.

He handed back the phone and lay down on the sand to wait, covering his eyes from the sun with his elbow. He could stick around Melbourne for a while. He could stay with John. The Melbourne Yacht Club had bands play most weekends, and soon he could even be feeling well enough to get in some dancing. Maybe he'd see about buying *The Cuki*.

"Dude! Did you see those mannequins on that boat?"

"Yeah, no idea why they're there," Buzz looked over at his fellow survivors. He couldn't believe most of their limbs were still intact.

Beach Jesus was slack-jawed. "Freaky."

#

Heddy McCoy is a recent transplant to the Space Coast of Florida after a twenty-year stint in Chicago. She works from home and is an avid reader of all fiction genres but gravitates toward fantasy and sci-fi. She  geeks out for live music, television, and movies. Heddy grew up in Central Pennsylvania, telling everyone she hails from Pennsyltucky. She is still a Steelers fan, though now cheers for the Cubs.

A "Capitol" Birthday

By Ashley McGrath

My 20th birthday was capital in the excellent sense of the word.

I started my college education at Brevard Community College (BCC), which is now known as Eastern Florida State College. I became an active member of Phi Theta Kappa (PTK), an international honor society for two-year college students, in 2005. Later that year, I along with eight other BCC students filled out a lengthy application for a chance to be on the All-USA Academic Team competition sponsored by *USA Today* and PTK. Early in 2006, my schoolmates and I were officially named to the All-Florida Academic Team due to our academic achievement, leadership, and service to the community. For attaining this honor, we were invited to attend events for the Academic Team in Tallahassee, Florida's state capital since 1824. Despite being a native Floridian, I had never gone to Tallahassee before, so I was excited about this trip.

On Wednesday, April 5, my parents and I drove more than 300 miles from Palm Bay to our hotel near the Capitol. Later that afternoon, a reception with light hors d'oeuvres was held for the All-Florida Academic Team at Florida State University (FSU). Following the reception was the awards ceremony, where team members received medallions, which resembled Olympic medals. I also received a scholarship for my next school, the University of Central Florida. It was an honor to be recognized for academic excellence. My schoolmates and I were then treated to dinner at a steakhouse by our college's president Dr. Thomas Gamble whom I had never met. Dr. Gamble was a sociable man, and I enjoyed conversing with him throughout the evening.

Around 9:00 a.m. on Thursday, April 6 (my birthday), a beautiful day in Florida, the All-Florida Academic Team convened at the Museum of Art and Science/Tallahassee Community College Capitol Center, where we partook of pastries. The PTK Florida regional coordinator gave us instructions and an overview of the morning's activities. Someone told the coordinator it was my birthday, so everyone sang "Happy Birthday" to me. After we went outside, my schoolmates set off party poppers, sending confetti on me, and gave me a birthday card they all signed.

With my fellow team members, I made my way in my power wheelchair to the Capitol, a 22-story building located behind the old Capitol, which was turned into a museum. We listened to a speech by Lieutenant Governor Toni Jennings, the first female lieutenant governor in Florida. Governor Jeb Bush was not present, but I met him three years before at a disability conference in Orlando. Lieutenant Governor Jennings graciously posed with the All-Florida Academic Team for a group photo. We then observed part of a House of Representatives session from seats in the upper level. During the session, April 6, 2006, was proclaimed "Phi Theta Kappa Day" in Florida. (I suppose it would've been too much to ask the Representatives to proclaim

April 6 "Ashley McGrath Day." Oh, well, maybe next time!) I wasn't a political science major, but as a voter, it was interesting to observe the legislative process in person.

After the activities ended and I said goodbye to my schoolmates, I met a high school classmate who was attending FSU at the time for lunch in the Capitol's cafeteria. It was enjoyable to catch up and discuss our college experiences, which were different due to the sizes of our schools. My parents and I left Tallahassee after lunch and made it home before bedtime.

My Academic Team Medallion

(Photo by Ashley McGrath)

I'm thankful I had the opportunity to spend my 20th birthday in such a unique and memorable way. I had never felt so proud to be a Floridian.

# # #

Ashley McGrath is a quality analyst for the call-monitoring company J.Lodge. Born and raised in Brevard County, Ashley has a master's degree in Applied Sociology from the University of Central  Florida. She published her autobiography *UnabASHed by Disability* (available on Amazon and Kindle) in 2014. Ashley's writing was included in six other anthologies. She maintains a blog at unabashedbydisability.blogspot.com. Ashley is Treasurer of the Space Coast Writers' Guild, a motivational speaker, and a volunteer at her church.

THE SILVER KINGS

By Richard McNamara

My name is Mac, and here I am sitting on the hard bench of this snorkel boat trying to figure out how I had gotten myself into this situation. "Oh yeah!" I thought. "I asked for it."

Just a few weeks before I had asked my youngest daughter, Christie, what she wanted for her graduation, and without hesitation she replied, "I want to go to Key West and stay at the Galleon, and I want to take a few friends with me."

So, it's now a few weeks after graduation, and here I am in Key West with my wife and daughter and seventeen of her best friends from high school for a grand total of eighteen. Eighteen teenaged boys and girls, just out of school, all thinking they are all grown up and ready to take life by the horns. I had my hands full.

The snorkel boat we were on was headed for a dive and snorkel spot called the Eastern Dry Rocks about 6 miles southwest of Key West. I was acting as chaperon for my daughter and sixteen of her friends. All but one of our group had wanted to go snorkeling, as that was one of the things they wanted to do, so here we are. We were not very far out when Christie yelled across the boat, "Dad! Look off the starboard rail! Tarpon!"

I rushed to the rail, along with almost everyone else on board, and watched as thirty or more Tarpon rolled and cavorted in the water next to the boat. The sight of these large fish moving through their liquid environment is one of the most exhilarating things a human can experience while on or in the water. Watching these magnificent creatures gliding along almost effortlessly while we, on the other hand, kick, thrash, and struggle in the water is amazing.

I'm not sure if the Captain moved the boat closer to the school or if they were drawn to the boat, but we were less than 20 feet from them. These fish were all between 4 and 6 feet long and were as boisterous as a group of boys on the playground. As they rolled next to the boat, their large silvery scales would reflect the sunlight with a great flash of light. It was a sight to behold. We continued to enjoy their antics until the boat eventually passed them. They were now behind us, but as we all returned to our seats, we could still see them off the stern rolling and slashing the water with their tails. Who would have guessed their destination was the same as ours.

As we approached the reef, the Captain came on the PA system and explained that the Eastern Dry Rocks is a coral reef that is laid out in sort of a star pattern. There is a central hub with coral 'fingers' radiating out from the center. This forms canyons with coral walls on both sides and provides homes for a myriad of sea creatures from lobster to reef fish of all types, colors, and sizes. The center of the hub is just awash with some of these canyons 30 to 40 feet deep. The boat tied up to one of the mooring buoys and the Mate started passing out gear and giving us all instructions on the use of the buoyancy vests and what to do and not do once we were near the reef. The two main instructions were don't touch the coral and don't stand on the coral.

As soon as the Mate finished his spiel, I slipped off the dive platform and moved around the side of the boat, so I could watch all of my charges enter the water. Once they were all in the water, we headed out toward the reef. I stayed behind everyone just on the surface so that I could keep an eye on our entire group. We were about halfway up one of the canyons headed toward the central hub when the school of Tarpon that we had passed swooped in underneath us. They were acting just as crazy as they were when we saw them earlier, rolling, darting this way and that, and generally terrorizing the reef. The citizens of the reef were darting into their holes and crevices to avoid becoming lunch for these crazy guys.

I was mesmerized by their beauty. The filtered sunlight was flashing off of their silver scales as they rolled and darted in and out of my field of view. I now understood why they are called Silver King Tarpon. My awe was shattered by a great thrashing in the water just to my left. This was followed by a muted noise that sounded like screaming. I righted myself and stuck my head out of the water to hear, "SHARK!"

I looked around to see Jenna, one of the girls in my group, thrashing the water and screaming at the top of her lungs. I started swimming toward her all the while hollering at her to stop yelling. "Jenna!" I hollered. "They're not sharks! Stop yelling! Swim over here to me." I yelled at her several times, but she didn't stop.

I was almost to her when she climbed on another

girl's back desperately trying to get out of the water. The girl she was on top off was Nyree, another of our group. She was being forced underwater and was having trouble getting to the surface to get a breath of air. When I got there, I tried to drag Jenna off of Nyree, but she was so scared she even started clawing me. After scratching my face and shoulders, she finally slid off the girl and began swimming toward the boat as fast as she could, still screaming.

The whole time this is unfolding many of the other swimmers were also panicking as they thought someone was being attacked by a shark, a lot of them were even climbing up onto the coral to get out of the water, doing damage to the reef that would take years to regrow. There were several other dive boats tied up around the reef, and as I looked there were Captains and Mates in the wheelhouses yelling into their PA's, "Get off the reef! There is no shark. They are Tarpon. Get off the reef." Some of the crew had climbed up on top of the wheelhouse of their boat with rifles just in case there was a shark. Unfortunately, the reef was being damaged because people were so scared they were standing on it, too afraid to get back in the water.

Meanwhile, Jenna had made it back to our boat and was climbing onto the swim platform still screaming in a panic. I got back to the boat just as the Captain jumped down from the wheelhouse and tried to quiet her down, but she fought him off and went into the cabin running around until, finally, she went into the head where you could hear her crying.

I got back in the water and swam back to our group

to check on Nyree. Even though Jenna tried to use her as a raft, she said she was okay. I looked at her and saw that she was fine, except for, like me, some scratches, so we moved on into the canyon to finish our dive. Meanwhile, the reef was still being harassed by the Tarpon. Then, as quickly as they came, the Tarpon disappeared into the somewhat cloudy water of the Florida Straits. As they swam off the reef the other swimmers saw them leave, so they re-entered the water, although some did go directly back to their boats. The serenity returned to the reef, and our party continued their explorations.

Tarpon (Image courtesy Judy McNamara)

After a while, the boat captains started sounding their horns to call the snorkelers back to their respective boats. This was when I had my own little adventure with a denizen of the deep. When I got to the boat, I once again swam to the side of the dive platform where I could do a head count to make sure we hadn't lost anybody. I blew a little air into my buoyancy vest and was floating next to the boat when I got this feeling that I wasn't alone. I ducked my head in the water, and as I turned to look to my right, there was a barracuda about three feet away sizing me up for dinner. They are terrifying creatures, and this one was at least five feet long with his mouth slightly agape with those great big teeth visible as he hung unmoving in the water. His only movement was the rhythmic motion of his gills slowing pulling water across his gill plates, and a slow, almost imperceptible wag of his tail, which allowed him to hold station in the barely perceptible current. In my mind I envisioned him salivating as he sized up the possible meal just in front of him. I decided that the best way to handle this was to go toward him. As I moved, he moved with me. "Now what do I do?" I thought.

I swam back to the boat, and he followed me. I tried to swim at him again, same scenario. If I moved, he moved, always staying just out of reach. I decided to ignore him and went back to counting heads. About the time everyone was back, Christie swam over and said, "You gonna' get on board?"

"Just as soon as everyone in our group gets on, there's two not come in yet. I have this one little problem." I said.

"What's that Dad?"

"Stick your head in the water and look about three feet off my right shoulder."

She did as I asked and came up sputtering. "Oh man, what a big 'cuda. What's he doing?"

"Sizing me up for dinner. He's been there since I came back from the reef. I tried to scare him off, but he don't scare."

"What'cha gonna do?"

I shrugged and said, "Just go ahead and get on board and tell the Mate. Maybe he has an idea."

She got on board just as the last of our group got to the dive platform. I figured the time when I was getting out of the water would be the scariest because I wouldn't be able to see him if he tried to go after me. As I started toward the ladder, the big 'cuda followed. When I stepped on the ladder, the Mate was there with the big gaff hook. "Come on board slowly, and if he starts toward you, I'll chase him off with the hook. He's here all the time, and he's never hurt anyone, yet."

Great! I liked the YET part, but I got on board, and as the captain started the engines the great predator turned and swam toward the reef, obviously upset he didn't get the big meal he was expecting.

As we were slowly motoring away from the reef, the Captain came on the PA system and explained that even though the damage to the reef was minimal, it would take many years for the broken coral to regrow. Just about the time he finished his announcement Jenna emerged from the head and came out on deck. She had settled down quite a bit, but the event still shook her. As she sat on the bench, her friends were trying to put her at ease. They were all trying to tell her that they weren't sharks and that they wouldn't hurt her, but she was still not buying it.

The ride back to Key West was somewhat subdued because everyone was still upset about what had happened on the reef. The Captain was especially angry because it was his charter that had been the cause of damage to the reef, but he was at the same time glad that no one had gotten hurt. As I enjoyed the ride back, I was glad to see that all of my "kids" had enjoyed the trip, despite the scare. They couldn't quit talking about all the fish and lobster they had seen, how crazy he Tarpon had been, and how much fun they had had. One pair even got up close and personal with a Moray Eel when they got a little too close to his hole, but the most talked about event was the encounter with the Tarpon. These magnificent fish had surrounded many of them, and in some cases, even pushed and shoved by them as they tore around the reef.

Several weeks later, as I was still recovering from the graduation trip, I was reading an article in a dive magazine that claimed only very few divers get to see the Silver King Tarpon in their natural environment as we had. We had not seen one, but a whole school of these beautiful fish. It was truly an experience to be remembered, in more ways than one!

# # #

Richard McNamara's interest in literature and writing goes back to his earliest years. He is an avid collector of first edition books (mainly Florida mystery writers).  He attends several mystery writers' conferences every year. During his career in electronics, he has written many technical articles and papers and has used that experience to move into the field of fiction writing.

HOT HURRICANE NIGHT

By J.P. Osterman

My iPhone watch vibrated on my wrist, waking me up to a foggy, Sunday Melbourne morning. Yawning and sitting up to a cardinal's light trilling sound, I felt the long day stretch out like gooey taffy, a bit dreary and dull. Until I remembered I was going to the Eau Gallie Art Festival in the afternoon. Two weeks ago, I told my friend Andrea, "Let's go to it. This year is the first time the festival is at Wickham Park. I know we'll have fun, and maybe even meet some hot guys, right?" My husband died over two years ago; and this year, I've been, well, "looking."

"Sounds great," Andrea said. "And I'll bring some wine." We knew how to have a great time on the cheap.

I met Andrea over a year ago at the Melbourne Mall gym. With our playful personalities, we became instant friends. I'm 5'8" and she's a beanpole at 5 feet. I'm blonde; she's brunette. I'm somewhat of a planner; she's spontaneous. So opposite we are, yet so alike when it comes to having fun and laughing at just about anything. Once, we bought matching handkerchief dresses at Macy's in the Melbourne Mall and wore them to Friday Fest in downtown Melbourne. People told us: "Wow, you two look awesome, like sisters!" We dance and celebrate just about every occasion because, as they say, life is short and time is precious, so live it to the fullest.

I couldn't stop laughing as I recalled our street-walking experiences and funny-friend moments while walking outside to get my newspaper. I had a shocking surprise. The For Sale sign three doors down was gone. The place had been on the market for six months. I wondered, who bought it? A family as a starter-upper, or snowbirds? Glancing at the tall shrubs, spindly pines, and palmettos in the east, I couldn't help but notice the morning sneaking past me. Blinding sunshine spit strips of yellow fog into the smells of musty grass and blue ice-colored air. I felt as if Mars' heat might strand me in the middle of the street if I didn't retreat inside and slam shut my door. Before retreating inside, I spotted my buxom neighbor, Jane.

"Have you seen *the man* who is moving into Rick and Julie's house?" The realtor says he's out of state but moving into the place in three months." She pointed at the house surrounded by tall palms, shaggy shrubs, and blue agapanthus. "He's staying in Melbourne for a short while to check out the town." She had startled eyes and a cutting tenseness. "Wait until you see him. I thought a family would move in there for sure. But nope, nope," she nodded. "You'll be surprised! Oh my, the neighborhood will *never* be the same. We'll all have to be *special* good."

I wondered, is this man a good thing, or a bad thing? "No, I haven't seen him, but I'll make sure to say hi to him when I do." I felt a bit scared, but I didn't have time to chat. I had a festival to get ready for, and an intensive makeup session to enhance my 60-year-old face to look like 55. "We'll all take something over to him to welcome him to the block when he does move in, Jane. That's the best way to get him on our side, right?"

"Oh my, oh my." She appeared to about to faint.

She had me worried. Who is this man? Jane is an Amazon woman, and the new neighbor seems to have scared her half to death. After Zumba at the Melbourne Mall gym, 11:30 a.m. church, and talking to a few friends, I picked up Andrea for the art festival. She lives downtown by a biker bar and lets me park in her driveway so we can bar hop or attend downtown activities like wine festivals and pub crawls with Gary. Pulling up, I didn't have to step out of my car to get her. She was waving me into her driveway with her string bean body and party-ready smile. I knew she had wine in her huge bag because she was clutching it in a way so as not to spill anything inside.

I shut off the radio and cranked up the air conditioning. "Hey, let's go!" I too felt revved and excited.

She got into the car, her brown eyes beaming with anticipation. "Let's go go go," she danced in the passenger seat.

"Party time, pal." Laughing and belting up, I backed up; and off we went to A1A. We cracked jokes while relishing the salt air and racing with a flock of pelicans gliding over the Indian Harbor Lagoon. After turning into Wickham Park, Andrea kept directing me. "Over there! There's a space. Or, look to the left, here! No, right *here*."

She's like the *worst* back seat driver ever. "Cool it. I *know* where to go, and I have to obey this guy who's directing traffic and telling me where to park."

"Okay, Ok," she said, sounding perturbed.

I sensed her over-excitement and frustration at wanting to get as close to the entrance as possible. "We're almost there. Almost there."

I had a memory of the gym, and our power-circuit instructor Michelle, and I laughed.

"What's so funny?"

"I just remembered what Michelle usually says as we move from one power-circuit station to the next. "Just one more minute... you're almost there... almost finished."

"Oh yeah," Andrea laughed.

"I try to whisper so that only you can hear me, 'No, I'm not there yet, not *yet.*'" I hit the brakes before my laughter could make me rear end the car in front of me. I breathed so deeply I thought I'd suck the water right out of my water bottle beside me. "We're here. Let's go."

Inside the art festival arena, vendors were bartering with people. Through the chatter, oppressive humidity and strong hot sun settled on the pavement in suffocating waves. The tall, white square tents looked like protective hats as Andrea and I dodged others who were seeking comfort, shade, and just plain old-fashioned small talk.

"I want to see the pet adoption booth." I scoured the map to find it. A few times, as we looked at some beautiful artwork and jewelry, we asked a few vendors for the location of the Brevard County Sheriff's pet adoption tent.

"It's at the end of the entire row!" Andrea pointed toward a long line of white tents circling Wickham Park Lake. "A *looong* way," she groaned, her hair flattening in the humidity.

The late morning changed to early afternoon dry mouth in the heat. Andrea pulled out our cold wine that tasted sweetly refreshing as white grapes. The promenade grew packed with passing faces and all shapes of bodies and styles in a wonderful two-way procession. People had finished church, and the crowds jammed in almost shoulder-to-shoulder. I smelled sweet-light caramel corn, roasting hot dogs, and smoking chicken.

"Over there is the pet adoption tent," Andrea said, tugging on my purse.

The white tent appeared so much larger than all the art tents, and a giant van towered in the background, a sure display of comfort for the workers, volunteers, and dogs needing new homes.

"That's definitely the pet adoption booth!" I almost jumped like a two-year-old, then wanted to sprint to the lines of dogs. I did outpace Andrea as I reached it, and I felt disappointment instantly. "They look like they're all pit bulls, *ah*."

Andrea became distracted by a vendor across the road. "I'm looking for a little box for Pixie's ashes." Her dog died last month. She began to walk away. "I'll be back in a few minutes. Maybe behind the pit bulls are other dogs."

"Ok, bye" I waved at Andrea. Feeling optimistic, I

meandered through a long line until I spotted a large black-and-white dog resting on a blue blanket.

A stout female volunteer with short brown hair sat beside the black dog with floppy ears and hound-dog long eyes that rolled up at me. A sweet pang of happiness entered my heart that to a delightful flutter. I felt an instant connection. But why? "Is it a boy or girl?"

"A girl," she replied.

I knelt next to her. She was speckled black-and-white on the top of her head and dabbled with white-and-black on the paws. I pet her with long strokes on her warm black back. A quick peace struck me in a calming wave. "What's her name?"

"P a i s l y," she spelled.

I kept petting Paisly who kept glancing up at me. Then she licked my cheek! Wow, did I giggle and sank my lips into her glossy straight coat. I could see the black lab in her, and definitely the hound dog side. I wanted to sweep her up and take her with me right then and there. I turned around, walked a little away, and called Andrea. "Where is she?" I couldn't spot her at all among the chattering crowd. I took a few more steps beyond Paisly, but I still couldn't see Andrea. "Darn!" When I returned to Paisly, a man had beaten me to her. He was stroking her as if announcing his ownership over her. I knelt down—Paisly between us with Paisly's head turned my way. "*I* want to adopt her." A rush of threat rolled off my tongue. How dare he intrude on *my* dog and me?

He had on a blue tank top and jean shorts. When I

noticed his resemblance to the actor Vin Diesel, I calmed me down, and, well, let's say, a warming sensation flowed through me.

Paisly lifted her head, and her ears wildly flopped. It's almost as if she were trying to tell me, "Hey, get over this hot guy and just adopt me *right now* for Heaven's sake!"

He continued petting her, his strong tan fingers gliding over Paisly's coat in long gentle strokes. "She's a beauty, isn't she?" His voice sounded on the baritone side, so inviting.

I looked for a wedding right. Not there. *Hmm*, but I wanted the dog more than talking to him. "Yes, she is beautiful. I love her eyes." I kissed Paisly's black-and-white V-line in between her eyes. "I'm adopting her."

The volunteer perked up. "Great! You can take her right now after you fill out the paperwork."

Andrea appeared behind the man who had a bit of a perturbed expression. "I can take Paisly now," I said, standing.

The man stood and folded his arms. "Well, maybe *I'm* considering adopting Paisly. I just moved here from Ohio, and *I* want a dog." He smiled as if opening a Christmas present. *My* Christmas present though. "You weren't here when I pet her first, so *I'm* claiming her."

I looked down at Paisly and clenched my purse to my chest. I felt so sad. I'd connected with her! He can't have her. And besides, she licked me and not this impolite man. Annoyance fluttered through me like the injustice I once experienced when a teacher added up my points incorrectly and gave me a wrong grade. No way was this, this, thief-of-a-man going to take *my* dog. Through a vying silence between him and me, Paisley glanced from him to me, and then to the hot blue sky. She grunted through her nose and put her head down on her blue blanket. She licked my ankle. "See? She just licked me." I gestured at my shoe. "Paisly chooses me."

With red cheeks showing embarrassment, the volunteer retreated.

The muscular man huffed and stepped back, obviously deep in thought. I felt the fabric of space-time stifle as he and I contemplated our next moves. Maybe he didn't want to cause a scene, or perhaps he felt a fist fight coming on and didn't want to test my kickboxing skills? Whatever the case, he turned a bit sullen. In his tan-wrinkled forehead, I guessed he was probably around my age, or early fifties at the most. Then, I noticed a conceding loss sweep over his perfectly sculptured face lined with what appeared to be years of work in the sun. "Yep, I see." He shrugged. "She seems to have taken a liking to you more than me." His smooth full lips stretched into a thin, slight smile. "She's yours." He said in a warm tone of voice.

A twinge of regret snapped into my overly assertive heart for how I had snapped at him. He had to have had on Chapstick in a glossy kissable sheen. I leaned toward him. "Thanks." I reached out to shake his hand, and he quickly grasped mine with a firm-hard strength. *Oooo*, I thought as I inhaled, and breathed again. Warmth and strength powered through me into a burning explosion of attraction. What a grip! He towered four inches taller than me and was what I call *gym hot-and-fit*. As our hands unclasped, he gave me a slow look over, apparently reading my face and body like someone desiring Oreo cookies. Or, was that just my imagination? My stomach groaned, but another type of hunger raced through me as I had never experienced. Can this type of magnetic attraction strike people out of nowhere? The poets talk about such desirability, and musicians compose songs about love at first sight. But come on! Now, here, at an art festival? Can this type of attraction happen to me? My heart fluttered in onset of disappointment. The guy probably can't stand me, or, most likely he's married, or, he has a girlfriend. Oh well, I'll probably *never* see him after this. My gosh, how come communication becomes so hard between men and women in the older years? Perhaps, if it weren't for this unfortunate little spat over *my* dog, I could have asked him some more questions, and maybe, set my mind on him as a possible date, or just came out and asked him if he'd like to split a hot dog with all the gushy trimmings at the hot dog stand. Darn it and drats!

"Bye, and good luck to you and Paisly," he replied, turning away, and slowly walking away.

"Oh my, God," Andrea blurted out through parted lips. "I think he likes you, Joyce." She pushed me to go after him.

I thought about all of God's great creations. Mystery Man is definitely one of them. "I can't." I stepped back, and Paisly lunged up almost as if wanting to chase after him, missing him.

She nudged me. "You have to go talk to him. He's so manly!"

I set my purse down next to Paisly who nestled next to my leg. "Well, after I fill out the paperwork to adopt Paisly—"

"You're adopting her for sure?" Andrea said in wide-eyed excitement. She clapped.

I knelt down next to Paisly—the loss of "mystery man" waning to a fading blue moon. "Yep." I couldn't stop petting her, and I kissed her forehead. "But I can't take her right now," I told the volunteer. "I don't have any equipment for her, and I want to spend the rest of the afternoon here."

The volunteer handed me several forms. "That's fine. Just fill these out and bring them to the adoption center tomorrow. But I need this form filled out to hold her."

Filling out the form, I knew time had not been on my side, and Mystery Man had long faded into the mottled crowd moving back-and-forth on the promenade. I could only hope to run into him by chance at some point, so I quickly cradled Paisly's face in my arms, said goodbye several times—once tearing up because I didn't want to leave her—and then motioned for Andrea to leave a pit bull she was petting to return to the festival. "Come on," I whispered, "maybe we can find him, or should I say, accidentally run into him somewhere." Andrea and I walked the circumference until 4:30 p.m. We listened to music at the bandstand. We fed gopher turtles, drank beers, sipped our wines, and revisited the adoption center at 5:30 p.m. The giant white dog van had gone. I never saw Mystery Man. My heart sank. A lost opportunity. I'd never see him again.

***

The next day, Monday, I adopted Paisly at the Sheriff's animal control center on Eau Gallie Boulevard. The afternoon sun shone warm, and the Melbourne sea breeze blew balmy all around Paisly, my son Andrew, and I as we walked her around the grounds and took our time bonding with her before signing the final papers. Paisly and her majestic black-and-white coat stole my heart, and I knew I'd love her until either she or I would meet our "end." I also realized why I liked her so suddenly. She reminded me of my childhood dog my grandparents had on their farm in Indiana. Dixie was smaller than Paisly, and she died when I wasn't there. I never had a chance to say goodbye. This was God giving me back my childhood dog! She licked Andrew and me so much in those fifteen minutes that I thought I'd had a bath. I told the receptionist: "There's only one thing I want to change."

"What's that?"

"The spelling of her name." As she typed, I said, "P a i s l e y. I want to add an e to her name, not change it." Poor dog, she'd probably had several names, who knows? On the ride home, Paisley howled. I felt so on edge, like taking home a newborn. The receptionist had given us a bag of donated food, a collar, a leash, and a beautiful blue blanket. I kept petting Paisley as she scampered along the back seat.

Andrew tried to calm her down and reassure her.

"Paisley, we're going to your new home." He had a beaming smile. I hadn't seen my son so happy since his dad died over two years ago. "I love this dog, mom." He kept saying while stroking her.

***

Three months later, as I drove into my driveway, I noticed several Melbourne police cars parked around the sold home three doors down from me. My gosh, trouble there so soon over there? I could see my new dog having a barking field day with the new rowdy homeowners on the block.

Nothing. No commotion. No noise. Just peace and calm.

Who in the heck lives there and what's going on? A neighbor across the street, Vicky, had a long loaf of something in her hands and crossing the street to their house. "Hi, Vicky," I waved. She waved back and knocked on the door. Keeping Paisley secured behind my closed-in porched, I peeked to see who would answer the door. I couldn't make out a face or much of anything, just a man who said, "Thank you, Ma'am, and if you need *anything*, please don't hesitate to come knocking on my door. I'll be glad to help."

Well, at least he appears to be polite and neighborly, I thought, watching Vicky walk briskly back home. Then, I had an idea. I'll do the same thing. I'll bake banana bread tonight and take it over to him tomorrow afternoon or night.

The afternoon summer day arrived as hot and humid as a Florida furnace that felt like 105°. I saw a moving truck in front of the house unloading furniture, so the new neighbor, or neighbors, had to be home. Here I go! With the banana bread loaf in one hand and Paisley on her leash in my other hand, I quickly walked over and passed a mover. "Are they home?" I asked a sweat-coated mover.

"He's in the kitchen," he replied.

He? Not *he-and-she*, but *he*? Oh, so maybe he's single? I sulked a tad. Or his wife or girlfriend could be at work. "Hello?" I called inside. "Hi, I'm your neighbor a few doors down." I smelled a musty smell and heard the sound of a chair scratching across the floor.

"Be right there," he shouted in a low voice.

Paisley barked, yanking on her leash in a gesture to be set free. A warning? A show of happiness?

Maybe she doesn't like the stranger and unfamiliar house. Who knows, she could be protecting me from an ax murderer, especially considering all the police cars outside his house last night.

Paisley darted back between my legs, I spun around—nearly falling—and the banana bread went flying into the dark corridor. A man jumped in front of me and grabbed my hand, and pulled me up, catching the loaf of cake like a lineman snuggling a football to his chest.

I ended up panting under his chin. "I'm so—" I gasped.

His blue eyes widened in a startled expression. "You!" He glanced at Paisley then me.

"You!" I stepped back to get a solid footing on his threshold and steady Paisley as the movers passed us by.

Oh wow, Mystery Man, from the art festival, standing *right* in front of me. I saw my housewarming gift, all smashed. I snatched the crumpled loaf out of his hands and fiddled with the aluminum pan to straighten out the edges. Crumbs seeped everywhere on his blue dry-fit tank top. "Oh gosh, I'm so sorry." Flutters of embarrassment moved through me, and I noticed his strong tan legs as I knelt down and began gathering moist crumbs on his checkered tile entryway. "Oh, I so sorry." I stood, and he held out a little wastebasket. His muscles bulged in statuesque shapes, reminding me of ancient Greek sculptures of powerful Spartan men.

"No bother." He chuckled, setting down the basket away from Paisley. "Wouldn't want her having dinner here yet, huh?" He had a sense of humor. Good start.

I wanted to hear more of his voice so I could go home with more of him to remember. Oh, what to do now, and what to say? "I guess we meet again." I laughed, feeling like a klutz. I'm not making a good second impression. "I'm Joyce. I live three houses down," I pointed to the right.

He began petting Paisley in soft strokes, and Paisley sat down in compliance, obviously remembering him. "I'm Doug Stevens."

I extended my hand. "I think this is the second time shaking hands," I said, smiling. Then, I noticed so much of the sweet-smelling bread still on his tight-strong arms. "Here, I baked this for you." I brushed off a few lingering morsels sticking in the hairs on his tan arms. "Again, so sorry. What an entrance I made, huh?" I giggled.

"That's all right. I got a vacuum." He shook his arms like a swimmer warming up his muscles. As tiny crumbs hit the floor, Paisley delighted in lapping them up. Meanwhile, passionate waves flowed through me, lingering in what had to look like glowing coals on my cheeks. I grew nervous. Looking into his blue eyes as he tasted a smidgeon of banana bread, excitement and fright burned in me. Why? What is it about Doug that's making me feel like a high schooler asking him to a dance? I had to snap out of this puppy dog emotion and show him how intelligent I am, which might be a little difficult considering I nearly fell on his chest and spilled sticky bread into his shirt and on his floor.

"*Mmm*, this is good." He pried off a piece and ate it as if he hadn't eaten breakfast. Then he licked his fingers.

"I'm glad you like it." I caught a few pieces as they spilled off his soft, smooth blush lips and hoisted them back into the aluminum pan. "Here ya go. I didn't mean to make a mess. I only wanted to come over and introduce myself, not litter your entryway with banana and dog hair."

He laughed. "Well, thanks, Joyce." After setting down the bread, he pet Paisley again. He definitely could pass as Vin Diesel's stuntman. Then, I thought of all the police cars I'd seen that could unravel the puzzle behind Doug Stevens. "Did anything happen here last night? A few of us noticed police cars outside your house."

He waved in a gesture of *that's nothing.* "I'm a Captain with the Melbourne Task Force. They're some of my fellow officers. They wanted to see my pool."

Two movers came up behind me with a large dresser.

"Oh, nice." I straightened my glasses while feeling a bit self-conscious. I didn't want him thinking I was a nosey neighbor. "I better get out of the way." He motioned for me to step inside so we could let them over the threshold. Since Drew had died, I'd never had a date let alone been inside a man's home. Uncomfortable and vulnerable, I stepped back onto his front porched after they passed me, Paisley yelped, and Doug grabbed my hand before I could trip over the hurricane shutter frame. "Oh, gosh, whew!" Now, I felt like a complete idiot.

"No worries," he waved. He leaned against the door frame.

His tan muscular arms and strong body exuded a masculinity I'd never seen even in Drew. What was happening to me? At 60? Did I even want this feeling? And what would become of us, living three houses from each other? Another important thought occurred to me before I could let my attraction juices froth into a full-blown smoothie mix. Uh-oh, and oh my gosh. I needed to discover if Doug is married or has a girlfriend. How am I going to do *that* before leaving? I had to take a big risk.

I'd start with the banana bread since that's what made me come to Doug's place in the first place. "I hope

I made enough of it." I pointed at the half-eaten loaf cradling in his arms. "There's only enough there for one." Suspense filled me while waiting for his reply. The aluminum tin had a reflective glow to it in the afternoon scorching sun, illuminating his face to a mesmerizing glow.

"It's just me here." He shrugged, nibbling on bread as the movers passed. "I'm divorced. Been alone for 'bout a year." He gave me a blank expression. "And you?" He stopped everything, looking at the floor.

"My husband died over two years ago."

"I'm sorry." His eyes shone a deep sympathy when they met mine.

"Thanks." I thought: Don't say any more. That's what your friends tell you *not* to talk about after meeting a man you might like—your children, grandkids, and dead husband. I was running out of conversation but relieved. He's single! Now, some future encounters *could* occur that might lead to a date, but I'd never ask first. "Well, if you need anything, I'm three houses down." I closed his screen door and wrapped Paisley's leash around my hand.

"Thanks," he said, adjusting one of the hurricane shutters in need of repair. "You do the same."

"It's hurricane season," I began, "and we all help one another get our generators ready and houses secured."

He appeared shocked. "Oh, that's right. I'd better buy one fast."

I walked down his walkway. "Now's the best time. If

you wait until right before a hurricane comes, generators will be hard to find. I learned that lesson the hard way. So now, I'm stocked up on water, canned goods, batteries, and flashlights."

"Thanks for the advice, Joyce, and nice to meet you." He waved and turned away.

"You, too, Doug." I didn't want to leave our conversation without some hint at seeing him in the future. "See you around." Walking home, a lock of sadness wound through me. Was Doug at all interested in me? When would I see him again? I didn't want to make a pest of myself or make it look as if *I'm going after him*. That's all I need, the neighbors saying "Joyce is *going after Doug*." Nope, no way. So, how would I ever see him again? I hate that people tend to gossip and don't mind their own business.

***

I walk Paisley at around 6:45 a.m. and 5:00 p.m. She's a big dog-girl and needs her exercise as I need my gym workouts. Two mornings after meeting Doug, I left my front door with Paisley, walking toward Doug's home. In his police car, Doug had almost backed out of his driveway. Oh my, how to talk to him at this great opportunity? I stopped and waved as Paisley's tail rapidly wagged.

His Charger cop car stopped, and he rolled down his window. "Hey, Joyce, how's it going?" His face was freshly shaved, and his prominent cheekbones appeared a bit flushed from what I conjectured a long swim in his pool. I remembered the pool. It had to be the only big selling point of the house, but smaller than mine. I could swim the length of my pool, not his.

I pulled Paisley close to me on her pink leash. "I'm fine. But I better get walking before the heat comes." I gestured toward the sun bursting in yellow-orange over a long line of pine trees in the east. "It's gonna be hot in about a half an hour."

"Works for me," he shrugged.

I leaned down to the driver's side and peeked inside. The flashing technology on his dashboard astounded me. "Wow, you have a regular tech center in there!"

He chuckled in a low voice. "We have the best." He perked up, and his broad shoulders stretched in pride. I stood up to leave. "We never know the danger we might encounter, so, pretty much everything's bulletproof and Wi-Fi secure when we need it." He gripped the steering wheel as a race car driver at a start line and slowly backed up into the street.

I couldn't help but stare with abandon into his strong face, imagining his powerful arms embracing me, his tan fingers on my waist and neck. I turned away to catch my breath. "Well, have a great day, Doug." I tugged on Paisley's leash to move on.

"Hey!" The brakes squealed as he stopped. "What are you doing Friday night?" It was Tuesday, and I hadn't made plans.

"Nothing."

"You want to have a beer at Chili's around the corner? Say, around seven?"

I rubbed my lips in thought. Perfect, oh yes! I didn't want him to see my excitement though. "Sounds good."

"I get off work at six, so I'll pick you up at seven, ok?" He exuded such command and self-confidence with his strong arm out the window and his fingers gripping the frame. I remembered Andrea's words, "Oh my, what a manly man!"

"Sounds great, Doug," I waved, walking away. "See you Friday."

A date, with Doug! Oh my, gosh! I jumped a bit. But, what to wear? My closet could be a store. My outfit had to be sexy and not too fancy – sexy, informal, and modest. Oh my. Once inside, I slammed the door shut. My hands were shaking. I glanced in the mirror to talk down my frenzy. Ok, I'm sixty, five-feet-eight, slender, fit, with light chicken feet wrinkles by my eyes. I'm no Barbie beauty, but I'm still hot, to the right man who'll see me that way. Maybe, Doug? I wiped my face, the makeup-melting heat weakening my penciled-in eyebrows to nothingness. I reassured myself aloud: "It'll be ok; I'll be fine; I'll figure out what to wear." I prayed, and then a solution bolted into my brain. Call my friend Tammy from the Space Coast Writers' Guild. She and I have shopped together at Macy's in the Melbourne mall.

Ring, ring. "Hi, Tammy?" Panicked air flowed through my breaths.

"You sound upset, Joyce." Her voice reverberated concern. "What's going on?"

I told her about Doug, how we met, and our upcoming Chili's date. "It's in three days, Tammy. What do I wear?"

She laughed. "Oh, easy. Wear jean shorts and a form-fitting top. You'll look great."

That put me at ease. "Thanks." Before we hung up, her voice turned serious. "Did you know, there's a hurricane forming south of Cuba?"

"No," I exhaled. All my preparations sifted through my mind. I was ready until I thought of my date with Doug. "Where's it headed?"

"It's projected to ride up through the center of the state." I've known Tammy for four years. She sounded concerned. "Oh—" laughter "—and they named it Hurricane Joyce."

"Oh gosh no," I groaned.

"I knew one day you'd cause trouble." She laughed harder.

More alarm shivered into my bones. "When's it supposed to hit Florida?"

"Friday night we should begin to feel its effects."

I huffed. "Well, there goes my date with Doug I'm sure." A crushing ache pinched in my stomach. I had dropped off Andrew at church early in the morning for Christian camp, and I made a mental note to call his cell phone to check up on him.

"You never know though, Joyce. Things could change."

"Yeah, I guess, but still, if Doug cancels... oh, *I* know. I can offer to help him with his shutters or something.

Whataya think?"

"Sounds like a plan, Joyce. Text me now-and-then to let me know what's happening." We hung up.

On Wednesday evening, I waved at Doug while returning from a walk with Paisley, and Thursday night he passed my house in his police car. We confirmed our Chili's date, but before he drove away, I had to voice my concern about the hurricane. Our neighborhood Walmart was almost out of water, canned foods, and batteries. People had gas stations crammed like ants moving over mounds.

"Doug, I know we have plans for tomorrow, but if this hurricane—"

"Hurricane Joyce, right?" His sun-bleached eyebrows lifted in a humorous gesture as he chuckled. "Are *you* a hurricane, Joyce?" He leaned across the seat, obviously to get closer to me. "I can't imagine a sweet woman like you being a hurricane," he laughed. His teeth were white pearls on his chiseled tan face.

I crossed my arms along the passenger window and dipped closer to him. "No, I'm not a wild storm. I'm *really* a calm person. You'll just have to find that out for yourself," I flirted. The inside of his car droned with techno-inviting intensity, and my internal passion meter pumped with excitement and hunger. But I had to get to know him before investing emotionally in him. After all, I learned one thing from hard experiences: attraction doesn't mean two people will get along and be right for each other. I did know one thing. Paisley liked him. If a dog has a good sense about someone, that's a good start.

Would that hold up? His illuminated dashboard droned with speed-of-light processing, and he called off a command through his speaker. "You ever let anyone ride while the siren's on?" I could feel my cheeks flush.

"Not allowed." His face turned sad. "But I *could* let you sit in the back," he slowly motioned with his finger.

I cringed. "I'm not sitting behind bars!" I laughed and backed away from his hot black Charger. He laughed and time stalled between us in a passionate linger as a voice from the station resounded through his speaker system.

"That's not for me, thank God. It's been a long day. I'm done." He paused, his eyes appearing to lock onto my wide-eyed gaze where I lingered Doug's inviting coal-blue eyes. Did I see a bit of hunger in his as well? Or just a natural pause, maybe to cancel our Friday night? So *many* silent communications exude in body languages that can be misinterpreted and make it hard to navigate the world at times, especially in relationships. Could Doug be reconsidering our date? I'd give him a way out if so. "The hurricane might hit us late tomorrow night."

"I'm ready." He gestured at his trunk. "Are you?"

I saw concern for me in his rugged posture. "Yep." I had to project strength and control. "But maybe we should rethink going to Chili's if it moves our way."

"Definitely." He asked for my phone, and I gave it to him. "I'll call you tomorrow afternoon."

At 5:30 a.m., I shot up wide awake.

Honk, honk, my radio blared. "This is the National Weather Service with a hurricane warning for the counties of Orange, Brevard…"

Paisley howled. I pulled her next to me. Outside, I could hear bellowing breezes. Peering out my south-facing window, I marveled at a bright cloud circling the waning moon. Cirrus clouds dotted the churning sky like white popcorn kernels, and the air had a cool tropical lightness. "Hurricane Joyce is on the way, Paisley."

***

Early Friday morning, I worked out at the gym. I kept looking at the time. I couldn't wait to get home and hear Doug's voice. I'm sure our date is over, but what else could I suggest?

One o'clock, two o'clock, three o'clock, six o'clock, seven o'clock p.m. The sky darkened to Brillo steel, the winds chaffed treetops, neighbors hammered at boards, but Doug hadn't called.

"I hope he's alright, Paisley." I put ice in a cooler and frozen milk jugs in the frig. "I'm sure he's out there somewhere helping people." Paisley leaped on the couch, snuggling down. "I shouldn't expect to be a thought in his mind at this sort of time." Actually, I did. I thought he'd *at least* keep his word, even a simple text.

After locking down and pouring a glass of Chardonnay, a knock resounded on my front door shutter. The Weather Service announced 90 mph winds. Hurricane Joyce was destined to reach Category 2 status.

"Hello?" I shouted.

"It's me, Doug!"

I could hear the front porch screen tremble as I unfastened the bolt and turned on the porch light. The howling wind grew treacherous; the rain poured down in deluges of shooting nails; leaves and branches ricocheted as darts. "Come in." Heaven was mopping *everything* black, green, paved, and concrete.

He had on a drenched black raincoat poncho. "You okay?" He shouted through the deluge.

"Fine!" He shut the door.

"Sorry I couldn't call you." He showed me his iPhone. "Battery died, and I had to help some people board up."

"It's fine—"

Craaack... craaaaaack...

"The tree's falling!" Strong gales were bulldozing the towering tree right toward my porch. I tugged at one hurricane shutter, and he pulled the two shutters together as my royal palm burst out of the ground.

"My God!" A giant thump resounded overhead.

"I bet it's taken out some of the roof!" I heaved, imagining how my front porch was now scrunched metal. Doug appeared trapped. We discussed his slim options. "I can't think of another way out, except the back." Dread at the hurricane's intensity wound around my bones. "But those pepper trees beyond my fence are dense forest and horse whips right now."

He unwrapped himself, took off his wet boots, dried

227

himself with a towel I tossed to him, and pet wagging-tail Paisley. After a few minutes, he put his hands on his hips in an expression of deep thought. "I don't think I can leave." He gave me an embarrassed blushing smile, looked past me, and his strong cheeks turned rosy. "I'll call the station in a bit to tell them what's happening. I know for sure that no one's coming here in this storm."

I took his rain poncho and folded it on the floor. "I have wine. Come on in," I gestured into my dining room, "and maybe we can figure another way out." But really, did I *want* him gone? I poured us wine, and we drank, looking out my south-facing patio doors. "No need to close these shutters." We walked outside. "The wind's blowing east and west."

"Can't feel a thing," he beamed in amazement.

"It's probably this way at your house, too." But past my enclosed patio, the wind was snapping pine tree branches, mutilating pepper vines, and unleashing yellow leaves like an autumn frenzy. Clouds rotated high in a purple mixing bowl. Pine cones and shooting fronds began struck my roof and house.

Doug's strong face turned serious. "I'm going anywhere except here." His piercing pool-blue eyes shone a strength and resilience.

I filled with hurricane desire, quickly turned away, turned on the TV, pulled out two lanterns, and motioned for him to sit down on the couch. I sat down on one side, he on the other. I felt icicle uncomfortable, and his straight posture exuded the same. I wanted so badly to talk to him about it, but words stuck in my throat.

Understandably. We were out of our elements. I had a stranger in my house; he was in a stranger's house. How would we ever get through the night and tomorrow? After small talk on the storm, his day, and cringing whenever I heard a thunderclap, lightning strike, or overwhelming noise on my house; I tried to think of a way to make us feel comfortable in this tense and trapped situation. What's a way to a man's heart? Food! I had stocked up on a lot, and I had plenty of finger foods, too. All sorts of passionate images flashed through my brain. We hadn't even had a first date. I'm sure, at some point, if I don't *stop* my imagination, he'll detect my strong attraction to him, right? Glancing at him, I noticed he had moved inches towards me. There was his hand, a foot away on the top of the couch, so strong and manly. His short-sleeve Polo shirt fit tight around his tan biceps that looked like rocks. I imagined his hands on my waist, his fingers moving along my neck, his lips on mine. I gasped and coughed, and overwhelming awe overpowered me when I noticed his glossy lips in the dim yellow Tiffany light. Oh God, how am I ever going to get to sleep

"What's wrong?" He turned toward me, his chest beating right in front of me.

I put my hands on my tight, light-blue t-shirt and beat the fabric to loosen up some of the heat. "Just thinking about the sleeping arrangements."

"Yes," he coughed.

"You can sleep here on the couch." I checked my watch.

He coughed in an uncomfortable tone. "Sounds fine. Sorry, 'bout all this."

I winced. "It's not your fault that my tree almost fell on you."

We laughed.

"You mean, you didn't do that on purpose?" He sipped his wine.

I would taunt him. "Well, yeah, I guess I did. Right when your feet hit the door, my extrasensory perception concentrated real hard, and those roots tore up right outta the ground." We laughed again, his low chuckle and my fast giggle cutting our uneasiness. "You hungry?"

The lights suddenly shut off in a circuit-breaking thud, but then flashed back on, startling me. I could hear one of the pool's solar panels on my roof lightly bobbing every time a wind shear struck my house. "Ah!" I dashed to the kitchen table. "I hope the panels don't go flying off!"

"Expect more of the same thing through tomorrow." He walked next to me in the kitchen. "I can only imagine what's going on at my place, but then again, I shut off everything this morning." Calmness in his voice and his gentle manners put me at ease. He pet Paisley, and she left him to lap up water. "Anyway, back to what you asked me before," he pointed at the kitchen light that fluttered. "You bet I'm hungry," he clapped, "so what can I help ya fix?"

After offering him chicken soup, chicken salad, and

eggs, we decided on omelets. He whisked the eggs and seasoned them while I melted the butter and readied the toaster. Every now-and-then, I looked him over from head to toe. My heart fluttered. My hands broke out in a light sweat. Then, I turned uneasy. My dead husband never helped me in the kitchen, so I fought off every compulsion to offer to help. I kept ordering myself: Just shut up, let the guy do things his way, and give him credit for knowing how to cook a darn egg!

He poured the eggs in the sizzling frying pan. "I prefer being here like this with you rather than sitting opposite you at Chili's," he chuckled softly into my ear.

I lifted my shoulder through the tickle. "I'm glad you're here, too." I buttered the toast and leaned into his side in a playful move as he flipped the omelet and tossed in Cheddar cheese.

He put the omelet on his plate and divided it with the spatula. "Half for you."

Watching his motions as I buttered the toast, I imagined his hands touching my arms, face, and neck. I gulped down some wine. 'Thanks, Doug."

He slid next to me. I turned off the stove. He bent down, so we were face-to-face.

I knew I had to be smiling, staring uncontrollably into his coal-blue eyes.

"In spite of the whole tree ordeal, I'm glad I'm getting to know you, Joyce." He breathed with a deep penetrating rush of air. "I like you."

I had to take a risk. I put my lips two inches from his.

"I like you." I pulled away from him, grabbed my plate, and sat down at the table. He followed. I still wondered what we'd do for hours to occupy our time.

Tom Sorrells, a Channel 6 meteorologist, appeared on-screen. "Hurricane Joyce is now a Category 3 and approaching the Florida Keys."

"We're *definitely* going to be holed up here for a while." I sipped my wine and handed him a napkin.

He tapped his short's pocket. "I gotta make that call, but I'll do it later. I wanna make sure they know I'm not, well—" He laughed and leaned back— "trapped by some crazy lady who axed her tree down to keep me here."

"Oh, you." I whipped my napkin on his shoulder.

"I'm joking." He sipped his wine and then turned serious as he gazed into my eyes like a long poetic pause. "I really like you. I think you're a nice woman."

The kitchen around me morphed into a spell-binding curtain. His tan Spartan face appeared to glow with attraction. I couldn't speak, and it was way too early for a kiss.

"Yep, I'm glad I'm here. Wouldn't wanna be anywhere else right now." He looked down. "I hope I'm not being too forward."

My heart pounded. "No, you're not. You're being honest. I like that." If my voice could be a color, I would have named it rushing blue. "I'm feeling the same way about you." After eating, we put our plates in the sink. An uncomfortable silence drifted between us and into the living room as Paisley finished her dog food. I had to think of *something* for us to do, or else, passion would entice one of us to make an inappropriate first move. We had hours! The time was 11:25 p.m. I noticed playing cards and pulled them off the media shelf.

For two hours, we played Gin Rummy. Then we watched the news, all the while sitting opposite each other—he on the couch, me in my reclining chair. We talked and played a made-up game of *who could tell the worst joke*. Not noticing the time, we fell asleep, he sprawled out on the couch, me reclining in my chair, and Paisley stretched out on the cool tile.

The next morning, he was the first one up. "Hey, Joyce, it's eight in the morning."

I rubbed my eyes with him next to me and inches from my face. Paisley licked my leg. "Hi." I smelled coffee. Doug could be a keeper!

"I found where you store everything and thought I'd make breakfast." He touched my forehead and pushed back my bangs.

I brushed his hand with my fingertips. "Sounds great. Let me help."

"Where's Paisley's food?" He walked into the kitchen.

"In the pantry," I shouted.

I heard him pour her food into her dish and call for Paisley to eat.

Funny, a peaceful mood calmed me. Doug and I had gotten along so well. Remarkable, and what a coincidence: Mystery Man turned out to be Doug. It had to be a God thing for sure! There's something about knowing when the right one comes along. I couldn't say for sure yet, but I had a solid inkling that Doug Stevens would be in my life for quite some time. I'd only have to give him a first kiss.

# # #

J.P. Osterman was one of five finalists for the Patrick D. Smith Literary Award. She won a Rupert Hughes Award for *The Matter Stream*, now the Nelta Series: *First Communication. Battlefield Matrix*, and  *Astrocity Sagan.* Her one-act play, *The Man Next to Me*, won First Place at the Southern California Writers' Conference, now also *Pete's Crossroad*. Including *God Designed*, J.P. has written ten novels, one exploring Mars in *Cosmic Rift*. She released two short-story books, *Commuter Collection* and *Pareidolia*. Her novels include *The Screaming Stone* and *Corporate Revenge*. She is Vice President of the Space Coast Writers' Guild. Visit her online at www.jposterman.com.

THE DRAGONS OF VIERA

By Ima Pastula

As fate would have it, we were destined to become citizens of the favored state of Florida. Remember, Florida is a state of mind. Many changes prompted the writing of this small memoir to record the before and after of such an exodus and an existence did and done. Obviously for the edification of our descendants; in the event of our becoming ancestors, sooner than expected! Beginning with the inevitable; writing my way toward history and the sharing of such.

Morning light, the delight of a finished, well dreamed night. The sudden appearance of those dreadful, bloodshot eyes with a long tail; glaring from within the gentle waters of the lake! Am I awake? An alligator! Not what one wants to linger over morning coffee staring at from the patio window! Following every lurking move toward a tiny batch of ducklings; *oh my God,* that evil thing devoured those babies in one gulp! A virgin emigrant, in residences a mere few days, not what one wants to discover in the lake!

However, does one finally get their dream home? It isn't easy! The notice from the Town Council in Odenton, Maryland, that one autumn day, announcing the investigation into the use of the old, underground wells, surely dug before the Civil War. They were believed to be contaminated, and could force the owners of the oldest estates in Maryland to have the homes either condemned, or better yet, forced to have

235

city water brought through. Developers; over the prospects of the profits from the perfect location for development of said *Town Center* did and still does desire ownership of the land beneath the older homes.

Ours, over 100 years old, had all the favorites of ancestors: large porch, a half-acre of land, old weeping willow trees, the magnolia, and a grape arbors yielding yearly, batches of huge, purple ones. Of course there was the antiquated old furnace, the fireplaces, the ancient, junk filled garage and for sure a flavor of the old south. After six years of battle, fending off the developers; a truce. We would buy another house, close to relatives in Florida. In the meantime, rent our oldie but goody with the option to buy. Hired a landlord so to speak, he, a young man strong enough to clean the well, mow the thick grass, pick the grapes for homemade wine, and whatever else a grounds keeper does! Sold! Celebrated at the Olive Garden, in Melbourne, Florida; settling into the new adventures of becoming a Floridian.

Finding our dream house, yes, indeed, one we call our estate. Three bedrooms, high ceilings to help cool our mansion from the close to one hundred degree temperatures that invade Florida from June to November, when the hurricane season ends. All was well. Settling into the new was a year's challenge. The perfect house, readied for us; time to move in; family helped by ordering some needed furniture, like beds and such. That is when I noticed the patio cement seemingly moving! On second, third glance for sure, herds of tiny lizards were, still is, the movement seen!

So tiny, one would need a magnifying glass to meet face to face! Panic, don't leave any doors open for heaven sakes! It was a first shock that the alligators invaded our lake, actually when alerting the powers that be; panic caused a high pitched, trembling voice as I demanded, after contact with the housing authority by a hasty phone call "Help!" Indeed, I was told to call the *"alligator guy"* in a very non- panicked voice. Did that, still do, when needed, and guess what he said to me? "You are living in the alligators swamp, he needs his lake back!" Seems the development of Viera, Florida, sort of a suburb of Melbourne, was once a swamp-land, confiscated from wildlife to become a residential area! (Wild life still lurking it's confiscated homeland; one can relate.)

About those tiny, feisty lizards; becoming obsessed with the avoidance of them felt research would help with the understanding of the nature, favored habitat, and sexual behavior of said beasts. Did watch one, supposedly male, stalking a tinier one of its species; slowly approaching it from the rear, pretending to have his eye on a meandering ant, then the beast belched a red, under what I think is a chin, skin balloons! Appearing, as if he was blowing red bubbles under there, then flexing like doing pushups, with a swelling up of beside a long, switching tail! Don't you know mother nature caused that proficient, *what-ever*, to perform it's assumed mating ceremony, in its entirety, even though the wise, other beast snuck behind his array and escaped? Feeling like I was losing it over this obsession did refer to the Internet; not a good idea; seems the tiny beasts are the descendants of billions of years of evolution, they are *latter day dragons*! Not helpful, is it possible; a re-growth, a resurrection of their former selves?

***

Our new home, built not six feet from the biggest lake in the area, with a fenced in full sized, in ground swimming pool; we really were sure we had mustered out of the challenge of the kidnapped home in Maryland and soon were to become Floridians. You guessed it, on our way to bliss! Until that horrid night the alligator guy came to fetch the family of them out of the lake! Seems the old ones come out at night, the younger ones troll the clear water for their dinner! In the dead of night one could see tiny beams of light circling the lake, an eerie glow would land, at times, on a palmetto bush or the base of the squatty banana trees. Illuminating many times the docks across the lake, with small boats anchored, stocked with lush pillows and willow baskets. Lurking silently, beaming lights high and low caught one unsuspecting alligator with its mouth full of a small dog let out to do night duties! All told, of course, never let small children wade the lake side, or play near the water's edge. Then the clink as the point of a long stunner stick came crashing down on the pimply, green, knurled head of the critter, splat! He was stunned to capture mode, hauled off to simpler waters. A protected species in Florida, it would go on to breed another day. Actually the hunters bagged a family; two adults and two young ones! Stranger than fiction, some of the lake dwellers had paddle boats! Why would anyone want their bare feet paddling in the waters with lurking alligators?

One, finally, peaceful morning, enjoying the lingering nautical twilight, sipping from an unpacked china cup. Enjoying the aroma of a fresh pot of ebony sin coffee whilst viewing the scenery from my favorite window; a loud, squawking sound issued from the big screen TV! Alert, Alert! As the coffee cooled all in the area were ordered to evacuate! Indeed, our first hurricane as Floridians! Off we went, into leaping borders toward Georgia, half a mile in front of the worst hurricane ever, yes, nerve boggling isn't it? We moved among the masses seeking safety as we were, causing the prices of motels, hotels as well as private beaches to soar in overnight prices! Once adorable, now a motel room was at least , over $150 a night, one had to call ahead for reservations and could only stay one night. We became gypsies, wondering the southern states, waiting to do a U-Turn back to the aftermath.

The Invading of Neighboring States.

The deluge of evacuees crossed the borders of Georgia into South and North Carolina; not sure, really, how far *safe* was! Tempted to visit our old house in Maryland, but it was sold and too far away. The small towns, for sure, were stressed by our needs. The one error still a haunting memory; unable to get a motel, we spent the night in our truck, not bad with the seats lowered. When daylight offered some view; we had blundered into an orchard that some moon-shiners were using the trees foliage to camouflage the cooling, copper stills for the squeezing of fresh *white lightning liquor* (we thought, anyway) Thankful it was too early for the moon- shiners to be working, we backed out of the covey, dead branches crackling from the breakage, we squealed our tires toward a less occupied area! One day latter helped by a surprisingly friendly motorcycle gang! Whilst munching snacks in a small dinner; one such person approached, saying his aunt had a *Bed and Breakfast* place with a few spare rooms. We followed the gang within the fumes and roar of their *hogs;* to the nicest place to wait out the storm one could ever hope for! A shower, nice clean sheets and a feeling of safety! Noticing the helpfulness of those soon to face the very hurricane we all escaped from, felt the warmth of friendship with our surrounding states.

Returning, fighting the beginning surges of the hurricane that followed us and would soon threaten our very place of new safety! So close by, we felt the bulling of our sturdy truck, able to leap huge boulders but fragile to the onslaught of the monstrous winds, rain and destruction of force we were sneaking beside to return home!

Being halted many times by rescue crews, we arrived early morning to the half a house left. Raining, still, thru the non-existing roof; blown off, supposedly by the spawned, small tornado that also tore the mesh off the covered pool! The dumping of the flying debris into the highly chlorinated water, as well as changing the shape of the lake! All the expensive, close to new, carpeting felt like walking on water-filled sponges as we hurried through the destruction to see what had endured. Of course the force of the electrical outlets new behavior set fire to the dishwasher, the microwave oven blew up, electrical wires are all underground in Viera, so the current was left on to mangle and burn out wires in everything electrical! The beds were ruined, mattress full of rain water, bathtubs, overrunning onto weakening tiles. It would take hours to list the damages, so will shortcut to the ending. With great insurance coverage, surviving antiques, some small appliances, a few items from wardrobes undamaged as well as drawer items; went into storage for two years. Installation of hardwood floors throughout the house (no more plush carpeting, now rugged, water proof wood.) All new furnishings began to fill the renovation. The installation of metal, outside shutters, a preventative for future damages from the inevitable storms.

***

Back to living in Florida; one strange blessing from it all, even though the huge, steel garage door was puckered like a prune, we were able to restore our house with a new roof, garage door and all new appliances; of course small, monetary charge to us, using our homeowner's insurance policy. Just the anguish, fear, and destruction to deal with. A true blessing was, of course, the alligators with their sense of survival had fled way before we did, as well as the still small dragons, so told, dwelling underground till they felt safe. The weird looking, long necked, and long legged birds flew somewhere else and some might have refused to return. Mornings; during the recuperation consisted of an eager watch from the replaced, double glassed window from which I always enjoyed seeing the reflection of the full moon on the shimmering, star like sparkles crossing the lake and the in-ground pool. The new screen was soon in place, as well.

Only surviving natural objects between the lake and pool, a grassy six feet, was the banana trees, seemingly able to bend to the force of 80 mile an hour winds and torrential rains; did yield the tiny bananas right on time! As well as the giant Palm trees and palmetto bushes out front; did watch, just before we evacuated, as they bent almost touching the ground to pop up once again like a giant palm-ferned finger pointing to heaven!

Just a bit of humor; those long legged, long necked birds are a real hoot; one Saturday; a day designated *as garage sale day*, when tables are set out lined with great buy's for those looking for bargains; we saw three of those weird birds standing at one table, admiring the goods as if they were shopping! It was a hearty laugh that lingers; strange sight! Of course, the dragons were there also, but many acclimatized persons just stepped lively around them!

The fact that we reside in central Florida, close to the corner of the infamous *Bermuda Triangle,* hurricane warnings in force six months out of the year. The slow, nerve racking growth of the descendants of dragons as well as the scorching, summer's perpetual sunshine, the everlasting, attempted retrieval of the swamp by the aggressive alligators, I did make a new friend. Whilst early morning (before the sun rises full up) swimming laps in the renewed pool, a still tiny dragon watches. His head moving back and forth staring as if I were a tennis ball, possibly he does not realize he, also, is being watched, and one false move closer to the water and I am out of there! What really worries me is he blows his bright orange bubbles from his throat as he watches; doing his mating call? Or perhaps a call to battle? Weird! Still measuring their growth!

***

Must admit, becoming acclimatized has been an adventure, and native Floridians are fantastic people. Besides, it has not snowed since we left Maryland! You know, of course, after living in Europe, sharing the rich culture becoming acclimatized to speaking another language, returning to the United States was a shock to our stressed out human selves also! We bought our first house then, the antiquated one in Maryland; having been a type of diplomat for our government, being envoys of peace and offering a friendly truce it was a hectic life style. Following orders meant the soldier would be subject to war games (we think) absent from his family, many times for months at a time, you never knew where he was. So went the many years sacrificed to the government, the profile of a secret, CIA type of existence as well as keeping a sharp eye on your children as we were warned they just might be kidnapped to force secrets from our bonded mates!

It is not unusual to make friends with the once upon time enemies; we had one such sweet old Bavarian women, we called her Ohma (German for old women); she taught my youngest son, at the time but one and a half years old, his first words, in German! It took a while of night time studies to learn enough conversational Deutch, to know what they were saying. Having waited the demanded twenty five years before I could write this informative sketch about our tour in Europe, I now say it was a privilege to be the eyes and ears of our country, forever on the watch for any slip-up of the agreements made between Germany and the United States of America. Mistakes, especially in corresponding, sometimes were more serious than realized. Not only charged by the Bavarians many an American dollar for a chicken ran over by a tank, we were forever suspect. It was me watching you, you watching me sort of an exchange. (Sort of like the dragon and I?)

It was a relief to return to our homeland; however, many of the European holiday celebrations; the experience of a month's touring of Austria, Italy, and Switzerland made up for the interruption of our life-style in the United States. Mentioning this only to reveal the dream come true of during one's occupied times, before retirement; of the fantasy of living in a warm climate most of the year, able to swim your pool at Christmas time. Above all; the multi-cultured citizenry; having neighbors from the Islands; Bermuda one example. The musical , romantic sounds of the diverse languages as well as the exchange of cultures is that dream realized. Central Florida, after the trials and tribulations of become a resident, has proven a very exciting place to live; after investing in the many groups of writers, artists and offering to volunteer, it is a place I remain in; no more moving trucks, plane rides seeking better accommodations.

***

Having been an adopted Floridian for over 20 years now, indeed, it is home; however, still measuring, if any, growth of those dreaded wee lizards; for sure descendants of the ancient dragons. They have not resurrected as of date, and suspect they have now evolved to a new species of tiny beasts! Even though hurricane season begins in June, lingers until November; we have those metal shutters; creating an atmosphere of safety surrounding the house and, now, an adjusted neighborhood favorable to avoiding damages from the storms. In fact Florida just finished one hurricane named *Irma;* now recent history, *a really bad one, hit dead on,* after one really weird one; the mayor declared as the one when we "dodged the bullet!" Actually, it roared right past us, ruffling our trees, leaving tons of leaves scattering out and about the houses and a few broken branches; willing survival mood a *"no need."* If you are prone to thoughts you feel are wisdom, as I am, you will remind yourself there is no really perfect place to live! Here in Florida, life mends life; we prepare for the dangers, laugh when the trial passes and are forever grateful for the perfect days; which, actually overtake the dreaded ones.

Not to brag; but I have, after a fashion, quit measuring the dragons of Viera. Possibly just a dislike for darting, tiny lizards the cause for alarm? The alligators, the actual owners of Viera, are never welcome, just tolerated. Of course the pythons are given room to roam off beyond our sight and survival! Hardly ever encounter the wild boars! What does one expect? We are such a twin to the tropics; the jungle part of our living is just a natural state to be in! So happy to now, be, acclimatized and off to my favored window to notice the new blooms; actually, we have tropical plants that bloom year around. Living in this particular area of Central Florida is like a quaint game of *Russian Roulette!* This close to the *Bermuda triangle* we fake an aura of mystery; episodes of challenge and notice the hero's that defeat the threats into adventures. Keeping the metal shutters oiled, the doors closed to the curiosity of the dragons, it is a day of lovely sunshine, fresh bananas from the trees, and of course, a swim in one's own pool! Wouldn't enjoy living anywhere else whilst realizing I live in a paradise of sorts; enjoying the adventures and enduring misadventures as well.

***

Into the chapters; onto the virgin pages of the now infamous memoir, it will have content worthy of notice when finished. We will be ancestors teaching how one can change one's life; find solace in such a psychedelic existence within the surround of the myths and legends of such a flourishing state. Admitting; really, *Florida does become a state of mind.* The history itself, the early founding fathers, the creation of survivors, not to miss the overwhelming challenge of outsmarting the swamps and it's creatures; our one of a kind story of settlements and the defense of itself is legendary. Borrowing words from a quote; creatively profiling Florida's "State of mind":

The only State Florida
should compare itself to,

Is Florida of yesterday.

#

Ima Pastula is currently self-employed, a published author, and a master artist. After her husband retired from military service, they relocated to Melbourne, Florida to be close to their eldest son and family. Always  a writer, Ima now has 63 stories published on Kindle. She is a past president of the National League of Pen Women and a returning member of the Space Coast Writers' Guild.

THAT OLD FLORIDA TONIC

By Dana Weber

Sand drifted across Highway 98 by Gulf breezes whispering whims of new beginnings. Birdie had imagined the Cadillac to struggle with the bulk of the matching red and white Shasta. Thankfully, the winged convertible proved competent during that 1957 month of June when society was barely accepting of a woman hitting the road alone. At any rate, Eisenhower was improving the highways, and Birdie was looking to improve her mindset. A glamour gypsy, hell-bent on discovering her country while discovering herself.

Suddenly, a gust pulled the camper to the right causing her to glance in the rearview mirror – something she had avoided doing since leaving her cheating husband in Tallahassee. Seeing that the trailer was secure, she instead adjusted her white, organza headscarf along with the oversized sunglasses before another gush of wind caused an uptick in nerves and she tightened her grip on the large steering wheel. Mother Nature flaunting her Floridian prowess with harbingers of hurricanes.

"Bring it on," she silently dared. The thirty-five-year-old blonde had left considerably more trouble inland the moment she had hitched that camper to the Eldorado.

Earlier in the day, ancient oaks draped with long strands of Spanish moss formed canopies over the two-lane road running from the Tallahassee city limits.

Congested streets had given way to that shady back road which first calmed her anxious nerves. With those mossy, coaxing branches seemingly entwined in gossipy fashion, the monumental oaks were eager accessories to scandalous departures. Mockingbirds darted to and fro under the cover of greenery, chasing the naughty blackbirds away from nearby nests. It was then, after Birdie's fret subsided and her future took on new hope, that she had started to see in color. The subtropical portion of America's prominent peninsula was offering up its sundry charms and luring Birdie away from a life that no longer fit. The sunshine state would have none of Birdie's downtrodden attitude.

So, she drove on. Little did she know that the impressive oaks had only been a threshold to the open arms of a citrus country abundant with groves of cheerful orange and yellow spheres seemingly painted by Florida's steadfast sunshine herself. She slowed to take in the full blue-sky scenery with the top down as a farmer tipped his wide-brimmed hat to her from his field. The exchange had made her soul sweeter and crave her home state's fresh offerings just as a roadside market came into view as an answer to some of her yearnings.

Open spaces were abundant in that part of Florida and Birdie easily navigated her haulage off to the side of the country road. To a city girl from Tallahassee who had rarely left the confines of town, it was all so freeing. She stretched outside of the car and drew in the luscious earth soaked in salt air tinged with berries, pines, grapefruits, and oranges. The hem of her pink cotton dress fluttered around her calves, her manicured fingertips fiddling with the fabric belt as she strolled toward the farmer's teenaged daughters who patiently awaited her order under oversized eaves of the white frame shack. Green trim the color of palm fronds accented the rustic stand that also served as a resting post for a few haggard vultures, one of which spread her wings atop the tin roof. Additional feathered scavengers perched lazily nearby, paying no heed to anything that didn't matter. For mere pennies, Birdie was provided with a paper bag of oranges, blueberries, and neon red strawberries. A sack of Florida gold as far as she was concerned.

Birdie delighted in the juicy bounties while rolling along the backroad peppered with assemblages of crooked palmetto palm trees before farmland serenity was effortlessly exchanged for forested tranquility once the Apalachicola National Forest marched into view with her sentry of tall pines touching the sapphire sky. A different landscape had been introduced and Birdie's mind changed lanes once more while recounting the diversity existing in a mere thirty miles. The lost soul falling in love with the land's exquisite distinctiveness.

The woodland's fir guardians had watched her pass through their emerald estate until Highway 98 took over with endless vistas. The fleeting views tempted with glimpses of illusory turquoise water beyond mushrooming dunes. The sandy shore, however, did its best to compete for attention, often rising to sufficiently block the driver's view of the brilliant sea and instead boasting tall reeds bending and bobbing gently in the wind amid exotic clumps of sawgrass. Should the sublime coastal shoreline to Birdie's left be insufficient – which it certainly was not - the heavily forested land of the panhandle's national and state forests endured to her right. Never intimidated by the sometimes-angry sea, the grand pines often lobbing pine seeds to thrive among dunes. The natural landscape was wildly competing against itself while persisting to overcome the synthetic road dividing it all. Birdie's eyes grew tired from the never-ending photographic distractions and her hands ached from holding the steering wheel firmly to traverse the relatively narrow, sand-covered highway tracing the Gulf of Mexico's northern Florida shoreline.

The distant view was made hazy with heat, coarse salt air, and the resulting dirty windshield that the Cadillac convertible wore like a vagabond's badge of honor. Birdie craned her neck to see better then signaled her intentions while slowing to a stop, safely off the two-lane road. Ignition off, head back, eyes closed.

Relax.

Whether encouragement carried upon the voice of the ocean or her fugitive subconscious speaking out, it made no difference. She obeyed while the gulls cried out for spellbound spirits to join them at the water's edge. She casually followed their calls across the road with hands tucked in deep pockets buried in pleats. Reaching the dunes, Birdie removed her pastel pumps and thankful feet slid gently into grains of sand. One foot in front of the other – the mantra she had been repeating since deciding it was time to take control of her future; the recent past suddenly lackluster and faded compared to the vibrant trail of treasures discovered along the panhandle's thoroughfares. Over the dunes, moving forward in wonder and amazement.

Ahhhh.

Icy water refreshed sore feet finally free of their confines. Shells and sand worked with the salt water to massage them back to life as the sun began its descent. Birdie stood with stoical posture in the late day tide to take in the performance. Streams of pink and purple emerged then burst about until the line between air and water could not be differentiated. The fanciful orb engorged with its evening destiny. Birdie smiled in admiration. The Florida sun flourished gratefully in the moment. So, too, would this Florida girl.

# # #

Dana Weber has a knack for page-turning storytelling and grab-you-by the-heart character development. She is the author of two 5-Star novels, *The Tallest Timbers* and *A Gathering of Appearances*. Her third work  of literature, upon which this excerpt is based, is titled *West*. Her novels are book club favorites and she appreciates lively dialogues with readers. A Cocoa Beach, Florida resident, Ms. Weber can be reached at DanaThomasWeber@gmail.com.

ABOUT THE EDITOR

Scott Tilley is the president and founder of Precious Publishing. He is a Space Coast Writers' Guild Fellow. He writes the weekly "Technology Today" column for the *Florida Today* newspaper (Gannett). He is an emeritus professor at the Florida Institute of Technology in Melbourne, FL. Visit his author website at http://www.amazon.com/author/stilley.

Anthology Alliance

The Anthology Alliance publishes collected volumes of work edited towards a unifying theme. If you are a writing group, a non-profit organization, or a school looking to assemble and publish a collection of your members' writing, contact us! We also work with aspiring authors to edit and publish short story collections, memoirs, and essays.

Anthology Alliance is an imprint of Precious Publishing. Precious Publishing specializes in taking your writing ideas from conception to fruition. We know that your stories are precious to you, and we'll do everything we can to help see your work published.

All of our books are available online from Amazon.com in both print and Kindle formats. You are the author, we are the editor and publisher, and the world's biggest bookstore is the global distributor.

http://www.PreciousPublishing.biz/AnthologyAlliance

www.ingramcontent.com/pod-product-compliance
Lightning Source LLC
Chambersburg PA
CBHW021232250626
47155CB00008B/2977